Attainment's

Social Standards
at School

Judi & Tom Kinney

Instructor's Guide

authors Judi and Tom Kinney

graphic design Sherry Pribbenow

photography Craig Booth, Beverly Potts, Rich Reilly, Jeff Schultz

executive editor Don Bastian

ISBN 1-57861-155-5

Attainment Company, Inc.

P.O. Box 930160 • 504 Commerce Parkway
Verona, Wisconsin 53593-0160
Phone 800-327-4269 • Fax 800.942.3865
www.AttainmentCompany.com

An Attainment Publication

about the authors

Judi Kinney is a multicategorical special education teachers of 25 years experience who has authored a number of books for Attainment Company and IEP Resources. Tom is a journalist, author and video producer. Together they create the IEP Resources catalog and write and edit for Attainment and IEP companies. They have been married for 34 years, have lived on the same 13 acres of rural property outside Madison, Wisconsin for 33 years, and have two daughters in their 20s. They have practiced organic gardening for three decades and spend much of their spare time in the gym.

introduction
table of contents

table of contents

introduction
social standards at school
a student self-monitoring program

In a complex society such as ours, it seems an impossible task to assemble a comprehensive inventory of social skills—a social skill standard—that applies to all students. After all, "we" include people of almost every religion, race and background on the planet. How can a single set of social skill standards prove relevant for everyone?

The answer is by keeping it simple and recognizing the common need schools have to maintain fundamental standards of discipline and academic achievement!

While the social skill standards put forth in this Instructor's Guide will require modification based on school-to-school variances, the proficiencies taught here establish a fitting standard of basic social skills that are essential for all students to acquire to succeed in school.

The purpose of this program is to help individual students attain these skills and then link them to a set of standards of behavior for your entire school. Social Standards is for all students, particularly those who struggle mastering the subtleties (and demands) of behavioral expectations. And it's 100% inclusive. Every student should be aware of these skills and either already possess, or be in the process of acquiring them; that's how fundamental they are.

In addition, while the 53 skill sets provided here are designed to provide classroom standards for all students K-6, they telescope in on special education students and are ideal to write to IEPs. A further advantage is that by concentrating on classroom standards for all kids, it takes the onus off singling out special needs students.

While the social skills presented here are sequenced in a rough chronology and can be followed as such, each skill is really designed to be implemented individually as needs arise among certain students. In other words, If Johnny has been getting in fights outside the cafeteria, work with him on skill set #10, Standing in Line.

The fact is that social skills are being taught (and learned) in school everyday whether you guide their instruction or not: Why not be in the driver's seat when it comes to determining the direction that instruction takes?

purpose of the program

purpose

To provide structured, step-by-step training in 53 school-specific social skill standards.

audience

Students grades 1-6 who would benefit from social skill instruction.

program description

The Social Skills Standards program includes this Instructor's Guide with reproducibles for teacher and student use. All necessary lesson plans, data sheets and progress reports are found in the appendix. Filled out samples of data collection forms are given on the following pages.

This guide addresses 53 social skill standards that will vary little from school to school, yet come as close as possible to providing prerequisites for maintaining a polite, respectful and orderly school system for students and staff alike.

other social standards program components

While all components are designed to stand alone as educational materials, the Social Standards at School program includes in its entirety: this curriculum, a DVD, two videos and a deck of 108 Social Standards cards. The age appropriate actors and actresses in the videos and DVD are also represented in the photos of students in this curriculum. While this guide is a step-by-step curriculum, the videos and DVD model social behavior in action and provide a motivation for students to succeed in developing their social skills. The card deck is designed for large group, small group or one-on-one activities.

benchmarks, skills, sequences

Social Skill Standards promotes student self sufficiency by teaching five benchmarks which combine into skills. Each skill (e.g., "standing in line") is reflected by a single objective (e.g., "The student will stay in his place in line, keeping hands to self and using acceptable school language.") Each skill and its objective is a complete activity in itself. Skills in turn connect to form sequences. Sequences are skills that naturally occur back to back. For example, S practices Standing in Line, Eating Lunch and Going out for Recess, three activities that often occur in that order. You simply find the order of skill sequences that makes sense in your school. Once you establish a sequence, use it to form a student portfolio assessment that each student carries with her. *(The relationship between these three components is detailed on page 8.)*

these three components are:

---

benchmarks

1. S will stay in assigned (or established) spot.
2. S will stand with hands and feet to self.
3. S will be patient and move ahead with the line.
4. S will use voice volume cued by the teacher.
5. S will talk in acceptable school language.

Benchmarks

Five measurable Benchmarks to obtain the objective of the skill set. (Use all five or any the student needs to build the skill.)

---

standing in line
teacher guidelines

narrative

Students are constantly required to stand in line for one reason or another. This can be difficult for some and predispose them to inappropriate behaviors. For example, if the class must wait outside of a specials class, some students may take advantage of the teacher standing with her back to the line waiting to enter the lab. It can be a tempting time for some kids to become verbally or physically abusive to peers.

Other students who are impatient or have limited attention spans don't like to wait in a lunch line and will butt in to get served first.

Still others have body space issues and are unable to tolerate standing with people on either side of them.

Chatty students may find this an opportunity to carry on a social conversation. Loud students can interrupt teaching in other classrooms as they stand in the hallway.

Learning how to manage one's behavior while in line is essential because it happens so often throughout the school day. Standing in line also occurs in a community setting such as the grocery store or waiting to purchase movies tickets.

Review the rules for lining up and waiting in line at the beginning of the year. Reviewing social rules early for the whole class may prevent future problems.

Don't allow students to swap or change places in line once their place has been established.

objective

The student will stay in place in line, keeping hands to self and using acceptable school language.

benchmarks

1. S will stay in assigned (or established) spot.
2. S will stand with hands and feet to self.
3. S will be patient and move ahead with the line.
4. S will use voice volume cued by the teacher.
5. S will talk in acceptable school language.

problem checklist

Students who have trouble standing in line (e.g., a cafeteria line), or who have body space issues (e.g., a student with a severe attention deficit disorder) often act out when the line moves slowly. These students can manage their time better if they have a structured sequence of behaviors expected of them while standing and waiting in a crowded line.

teacher's script

Say, "Standing in line takes a lot of patience, but it's something you have to do a lot when you're in school, so you might as well get used to it. Once you have a place in line, stay there, keep your hands to yourself, move ahead as the line moves and don't talk too loud."

46

Skills

The ability to complete the objective, which is composed of five sequenced Benchmarks.

10
standing in line
student page

date _____
time _____
setting _____
teacher _____
period _____
student name _____
_____

self-talk story

When I am waiting in the line to get lunch I need to remember to stay in my own place. I have to respect other students and not let a friend cut in front of me. I have to try to keep my hands and feet to myself and not put them on the walls or lean against someone else. It is hard but I have to try to be patient and not get upset with those people in front of me because the line is moving slowly. I can talk to my friends in a normal classroom voice. We can talk about what we want to do at recess or make plans to do something together on the weekend.

M T W R F

self-monitoring checklist

1. I stay in line and I don't change places.
2. I respect school property and other people by keeping my hands and feet to myself.
3. I am patient if the line moves slowly.
4. I talk in a normal voice.
5. I talk about what I want to do at recess time or any other topic that is okay to talk about in school.

M T W R F

my story

Sequences

The combining of two or more Skills in a naturally occurring sequence.

23
lunch break
student page

date _____
time _____
setting _____
teacher _____
period _____
student name _____
_____

self-talk story

While in the cafeteria I must remember to stay in my place and to talk in a normal classroom voice. I can talk about things that are appropriate in school. When the line is long it is hard to wait but I have to remember not to yell at the people in front of me or push then to get the line to move faster. I take the food I need and thank the people serving the food. When my tray is full I walk directly to the area assigned to my class.

M T W R F

self-monitoring checklist

24
eating skills
student page

date _____
time _____
setting _____
teacher _____
period _____
student name _____

eating lunch

self-talk story

My friends like to have lunch with me when I follow the rules for eating. I must use my knife, fork and spoon the right way. I have to remember not to talk when I have food in my mouth. If one of my friends has food to share, I have to remember to ask before taking anything off of another person's tray. When I am finished I use my napkin to wipe my face and hands. Before leaving the lunchroom I look to clean up any mess that I have made while eating.

M T W R F

self-monitoring checklist

1. I use my fork, spoon, and knife correctly.
2. I eat with my mouth closed and remember not to talk with food in my mouth.
3. I ask before taking food from someone else.
4. I use my napkin to clean my face and hands.
5. I clean up my place after eating.

M T W R F

my story

67

69

long term goals

1. To achieve mastery of 53 social skill sets independently.

2. To understand the importance of strong and consistent social skills.

3. To use these social skills daily with consistency in a school setting.

social skill standards procedure

1. Assess a student on two or three related skills that naturally occur in sequence. For example, #10 Standing In Line, #23 Lunch Break and #24 Eating Skills. Your choices of these activities will usually be needs based. If a student is struggling with a given social skill, start there and build around it with adjacent skills. Or just start with one skill.

   Assess the activities as unobtrusively as you can in the location where they are performed. For example, waiting in line outside the cafeteria and eating lunch. Usually, you have done an informal assessment of this kid's social skills in these settings many times before and already have a pretty good idea of his needs. (In fact, you have probably disciplined him more than once for his poor performance on some skills.) This informal observation of the student performing the activity without his awareness of your attentions will provide you with a clear picture of his needs and will help you determine priority areas.

   Most of the time you will be able to observe in the course of the normal school day without going out of your way, since these activities intertwine with daily events.

   If needed, use photocopies of the benchmarks for each objective as reminders of individual steps during the assessment process.

2. Decide which activity to work on based on this initial assessment, and decide the scope of your intervention: i.e., will it be a few steps, an entire skill set or a sequence of sets? The extent to which you need to break down instruction into smaller components (steps) depends on the demand each activity places on each student.

3. If there's no need to simplify, teach the entire skill with all benchmark steps included. As the student begins to exhibit minimal competency on steps and sets, phase in use of the "student page" and the "self-monitoring" process.

4. At this point, the student begins to aid you in the data collection process. Compile a student portfolio, on which she will monitor her own progress.

5. When the student can complete the set without your help and can fill out her self-monitoring chart by herself, attach the single set to a sequence of sets. Use the Sequence Assessment Sheets and the Sequence Goal Form to document your progress.

6. Once the student can complete a set without help and complete his self-monitoring chart to 80% proficiency, he has acquired mastery and is ready to move on to the next priority area.

7. However, continue your informal observation during daily performance of these social skills to insure that she is maintaining mastery of them. If she slips, repeat the above process starting wherever you think is appropriate.

Three form types are included in the record keeping system: **Home contact forms, data collection forms** and **goal statements**. Filled out form samples appear on the next several pages. The original blank reproducibles you will use are in the appendix. Don't write on the forms in this book, since they're masters for you to copy. The following pages explain and give completed form samples.

Introductory Letter

This introduces and explains the Social Standards program to parents or caregivers and asks for their help where appropriate.

It can also be helpful as a script for you to present the results of this program at student conferences or IEP meetings. The top of the sheet is open so you can reproduce it on your own letterhead. Personalize by filing in the names.

---

resources
introductory letter

Date *Sept. 1*

Dear *John and Jane Smith*,

_____*John Jr.*_____ will soon begin a program called Social Standards in School. This program teaches 53 social skills that are important for your child to have to experience success and happiness in school.

Social Standards promotes independence and competency in such basic social skills as Asking for Help, Dealing with Bullies and Responding to Teasing. Complex skills are included, like Making an Apology and Accepting Criticism.

As your child makes progress in this program, he/she will be asked to "self-monitor" his/her improvements. This means he/she will chart his/her own progress on a form provided for him/her. Your child will carry these forms around with him/her as part of a student "portfolio." Sharing his/her forms with you can be a helpful part of his/her progress and for this reason he/she will be encouraged to bring this portfolio home to share with you.

Included with this letter is a progress report listing the 53 skills on which your child will be assessed. Each skill is made up of five steps, or Benchmarks, which will be included in the portfolio your child will bring home.

I appreciate any help you are able to give me.

Cordially, *Susan Jones*

555-5555
phone

home contact forms

Use the **Home Report** to encourage parent involvement and to exchange information. Once the student is working on a "student page" skill and has it in her portfolio, ask her to take it home to share with her family. Some of the benchmarks on many skills (e.g., "making eye contact") can be as easily practiced and reinforced at home as at school.

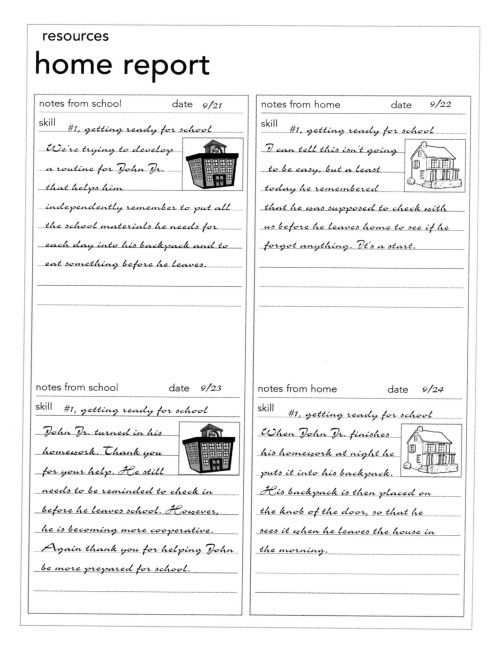

data collection forms

Begin with an accurate baseline to set attainable goals. As you gather data you can track student progress and determine whether your approach is working or if it needs to be adjusted. It also gives you measurable results for IEPs. And this data clearly tells you what the student's skills and deficits are.

To collect this information, Social Standards provides three data collection forms: Progress Report, Skill Assessment and Sequence Assessment. The following pages give filled out samples of each.

The **Progress Report** charts student performance through a semester or more. The key is at the bottom of the form: (+) S can complete the skill successfully and independently, (-) is still learning, and (x) already knows how to perform the skill and doesn't need to work on it. If none of these apply, leave the space blank. (Note: Send a copy of the report home with the introductory letter to parents.)

resources

progress report

student___John Jr. Smith___
instructor___Susan Jones___

social skills

getting ready

	date	rating	date	rating	date	rating
1. getting ready for school						
2. walking to school						
3. waiting for the bus						
4. riding the bus						
5. arriving by car						
transitions						
6. transition into the building						
7. individual transitions						
8. going to the IMC						
9. being in specials						
10. standing in line	9/5	−	9/20	+		
11. transition into specials						
12. group transition						
13. going to the office						
14. checking out of school						
classroom						
15. visitor to the classroom						
16. one on one						
17. large group activities						
18. transitions in class						
19. quiet time						
20. small group activities						
21. getting organized	9/5	−	9/20	+		
22. class jobs						
breaks & special events						
23. lunch break	9/5	x	9/20	+		
24. eating skills	9/5	x	9/20	+		
25. coming in from recess						
26. knowing recess rules						
27. crisis drills						

rating key: [+] can do independently [−] in training [x] can't perform the activity but not in training [ ] not applicable

resources

progress report

semester___Fall, 2020___
comments___

social skills

	date	rating	date	rating	date	rating
28. going to the nurse						
29. field trips						
30. going to the bathroom						
anyplace						
31. greeting teachers						
32. asking for help						
33. respecting body space	9/5	−	10/20	+		
34. responding to teasing						
35. being responsible						
36. making an apology						
37. voice volume	9/5	−	9/5	+		
38. accepting criticism						
39. respecting teachers						
peer relationships						
40. meeting someone new						
41. greeting friends						
42. joining a group of friends						
43. playing with friends						
44. starting conversations						
45. respecting friends						
46. being a good sport						
47. dealing with bullies						
48. dealing with conflicts						
49. compromising						
50. showing empathy						
51. following directions	9/5	−	10/20	+		
52. being compliant						
53. accepting others						

rating key: [+] can do independently [−] in training [x] can't perform the activity but not in training [ ] not applicable

introduction

data collection forms

Record on the **Skill Assessment Sheet** how students do on each Skill. Here, the Skill is listed at the top of the form, followed below by the five Benchmarks required to master it.

resources

skill assessment sheet

skill	*standing in line*			student	*John Jr. Smith*		

skill # *10*	date 9/10	date 9/15	date 9/20	date 9/25	date 10/10
benchmarks					
1. *S will stay in assigned (or established) spot.*	+	+	+		
2. *S will stand and keep hands and feet to self.*	−	−	−		
3. *S will be patient and move ahead in line.*	+	+	+		
4. *S will use voice volume cued by teacher.*	−	−	−		
5. *S will talk in acceptable school language.*	+	+	+		

rating key: [+] well done   [−] poorly done   [x] did not do   [ ] not applicable

comments   *While John Jr. tends to be loud and to be constantly touching other students when standing in line, he is well liked by most kids and they don't seem to mind. Nonetheless, he needs practice on this skill even if he doesn't get negative feedback like other kids do for the same behaviors.*

goal set *11/20*	review *9/20*
date	date

data collection forms

The **Sequence Assessment Sheet** is for recording student progress on two or more Skills performed in order. The key here is to sequence Skills that logically follow one another rather than following their order in the guide. Note that the book is not sequenced in this fashion, but is grouped categorically, so your sequence may include Skills from all 53, such as those in this sample.

resources

sequence assessment sheet

student _John Jr. Smith_

skills	date 9/10	date 9/15	date 9/20	date 9/25	date 10/10
1. standing in line (#10)	x	–	x	+	+
2. eating lunch (#23)	–	–	x	x	+
3. going out for recess (#24)	x	–	+	+	+
4.					
5.					
6.					
7.					
8.					

rating key: | + | well done | – | poorly done | x | did not do | | not applicable

comments _While John Jr.'s behavior appears to be more in control in the classroom throughout the morning, his behavior seems to escalate starting with the lunch break. John has difficulty transitioning from the classroom to the less structured environment of the cafeteria. He becomes more impulsive and has less control of his behavior. For example, it is hard for him to wait in line to get into the cafeteria and during lunch itself and by the time he gets back in from recess, sometimes he's out of control._

goal set _11/20_   date   review _9/20_   date

goal statements

After you have assessed students in the informal manner we have suggested—i.e., observing them during the course of your normal routine performing the 53 social skills in this guide on a daily basis—you are ready to begin an intervention. When you do an intervention, you will need to do it for two weeks minimum. With some students on some skills, it may take a month or more. This is in part because for many children, especially oppositional defiant youngsters, their behavior and performance on a given skill, as they mount their resistance, may actually deteriorate at first. For others, certain skills will pose unique challenges. To take an extreme example, a student with autism may never be comfortable "standing in line" in close proximity to others. In addition, students have to be able to perform at 80% proficiency before achieving skill mastery. Nothing less can be considered a measure of proficiency.

Objectives and benchmarks in Social Standards are designed to be readily measurable and easily observed in the context of your daily routine. For example, Skill #10 Standing in Line, Benchmark #3: "S will be patient and move ahead with the line." The instructor will typically be there when the students are waiting in line to enter a specials class or to go to assembly. Observation occurs in natural context. Though objectives and benchmarks are measurable, there will be times when they need to be broken down further or individualized for a given student's needs.

resources
benchmark goals

date *Oct. 15*

_____*John Jr.*_____ will learn to *be patient and move ahead in line*.
      name   benchmark

This benchmark is needed for _____*standing in line*_____.
                                          skill

It will be practiced in _____*any location*_____ in which it naturally occurs.
                                    location

Successful completion of the benchmark is defined by performing the behavior

_____*patiently waiting in line*_____.

comments *John Jr. pushes the child in front of him if he thinks that student is moving too slowly. We have started to work on this problem and while he hasn't made much progress yet, he seems to understand that he could do better on this benchmark.*

The **Benchmark Goals** focus on five steps that make up a Skill.

goal statements

resources
skill goals

date ___Oct. 20___

___John Jr.___ will ___stand in line, #10___
     name   skill

by ___11/20___. Success is defined by completing at least ___4___ out
   date

of ___5___ benchmarks. Presently he can do ___2___ benchmarks correctly.
                                  quantity

comments _John Jr. has shown some progress in this skill, but
before he lines up the teacher needs to tell him where to
stand in line. If he is not directed by the teacher, he
tries to move to another place. He also still
tries at times to put his hands on the back of the person
in front of him. He has, however, started to lower
his voice volume in the hallway and has stopped
trying to direct the other students in line._

The **Skill Goal** is achieved when the student completes an entire skill, like Standing in Line to a minimum of 80% accuracy.

resources
sequence goals

date ___Nov. 20___

___John Jr.___ will be able to complete this sequence of
     name

standing in line #(10), eating lunch # (23), going out for recess #(24), by
                          skills

___11/20___ at ___4___ out of ___5___ times.

These skills have been sequenced because _this is the time when John Jr. seems to
have the most problems_.

comments _John Jr.'s improved behavior when standing in line
for the cafeteria has had a ripple effect on him
throughout this sequence. Now he is less impulsive
during lunch and recess — not as loud and less likely to
get in arguments with friends. The result is that when
it's time to come back into class, he's often more under
control and the transition is much smoother.
However, he still cannot perform this behavior
consistently and needs more work on this sequence._

Sequence Goals involve completion of a natural sequence of Skills performed in the proper order and consist of any two or more Skills.

introduction

Instructor materials include a narrative describing each skill, an objective for improved performance and five benchmarks for achieving the goal. Benchmarks are set in a sequential structure, guiding instructors through the five steps of skill mastery. In addition, there is a "problem checklist" to aid in trouble-shooting the solution, followed by a "teacher's script" that provides the instructor with suggested language to explain the skill set to students.

The following is an example of a **Teacher's page** skill set:

---

forty-seven

dealing with bullies
teacher guidelines

narrative
Students should never feel uncomfortable about coming to school because of fears of being bullied, excessively teased, or harassed. Yet, many children at one point or another find themselves in a situation where they are confronted by a bully.

However, students also need to learn the difference between inappropriate teasing and actual bullying. Teachers need to determine the differences between teasing and harassment. Helping students empower themselves helps build skills for learning how to deal with confrontations. Teaching children to stick up for themselves, to walk towards a group of friends, use good judgment when alone with a bully, telling an adult as soon as soon as possible, and getting out of the bullies' way are strategies which can help.

It is worth considering peer mediation if it is available in your district.

objective
When confronted by a bully the student will develop and implement a strategy for dealing with the bully.

benchmarks
1. S tells an adult about the times that he/she is bullied.
2. S develops a strategy with a trusted person to deter the bully.
3. S practices the strategy with a trusted person. (Walks with confidence, avoids being alone with the bully tells an adult when he/she is bullied and uses humor to deflect threats.)
4. S uses the strategy.
5. S assesses the success and modifies the strategy if necessary.

problem checklist
Often a teacher needs to confront the bully and find out the reasons why it is occurring. In extreme cases, administrators and parents may need to be involved. Once the teacher has an understanding of the situation, a plan can be developed and practiced with the child who is trying to avoid being bullied.

In addition, consequences need to be developed for the child who continues to bully because no one has the right to make someone else feel unsafe. Bullies need to be taught more appropriate ways of interacting with other people.

It also must be noted that interventions serve the bully as well as his victim, since bullies are often marginalized by their antisocial behavior. Role play rehearsals of the student's plan, both with adults and with a peer (usually a friend of the child) help to strengthen the efficacy of child's strategy.

teacher's script
Say, "Nobody likes to be bullied, but it happens a lot at school so you may need to have a plan to deal with it. If it's happening to you, you can tell an adult you trust and ask for help. There are some simple things you can do with a good plan that will protect you."

128

---

student's page

The student page is picture-based and designed to reinforce skill mastery from the child's perspective. It begins with a "self-talk" script that explains the reasons why a student would benefit from mastering the skill. (Note: Self-talk is defined as: The process by which a student is taught to remind (or talk to) themselves to correct some previously negative patterns of behavior or thought.) Following the script are the five steps the student must master, corresponding to the five instructional steps on the teacher's page. Finally, there is a segment called "My story" that allows the teacher to individualize information that may be specific, and different for each student. My Story provides a place for the instructor to individualize benchmarks for students as needed.

self-monitoring

This key element of the Social Standards program has been designed for two reasons:

1. to put responsibility for their social behavior in the hands of students,

2. to allow instructors to fade involvement with students as they begin to take responsibility for their own social behavior.

It's challenging to put a self-monitoring program together. The problem that predictably arises is student accountability.

Students must be taught to take ownership of their own record keeping and develop a critical sense of self-evaluation. While this may seem a daunting undertaking, once students experience success filling in their own charts they'll be off and running.

Children need to be taught appropriate social skills in the same way they are taught academic concepts. In order for a child to learn appropriate skills she has to be given both the information about correct ways of behaving and a sufficient chance to practice those skills to proficiency.

The following is an example of a **Student page:**

47

dealing with bullies
student page

date _____

time _____

setting _____

teacher _____

period _____

student name _____

_____

self-talk story

I feel uncomfortable and anxious whenever I see a bully because it makes me feel unsafe. I talked to my teacher and we thought of a plan to deal with it. I practiced the plan with my teacher and a friend. If the plan doesn't work, I will get help to make another plan until I find one that does.

M T W R F

self-monitoring checklist

1. I tell a friend or adult.

2. I make a plan to deal with it.

3. I practice my plan.

4. I use my plan.

5. If it doesn't work, I make another plan.

M T W R F

my story

_____

_____

_____

_____

_____

129

introduction

Often teachers complain about students with poor social behavior. This seems to be especially true of children who are in special education classes because of emotional disabilities. It is more convenient to blame the child or the family for a lack of appropriate behavior. Teachers need to remember that a child spends many hours during his developmental years inside a school building. It is far more efficient to teach that child appropriate social skills rather than to spend the time disciplining that student.

A typical response to shaping appropriate social behavior is to develop point systems with rewards and consequences attached to particular behaviors. However, current research has indicated that point systems have very little effect on making permanent changes in a child's behavior. Point systems seem to be more rewarding for the teacher than they are for the child for whom the reward system was designed. Alfie Kohn in his book **Punished By Rewards** notes that the more a child is controlled in a classroom the more he needs to be controlled and the less chance he has to take responsibility for his own learning.

Self-monitoring is a way to teach a child how to be responsible for her own behavior. The teacher who says a child cannot self-monitor has not taken the time to teach her how to regulate her own behavior and to follow social codes for appropriate behavior in school.

Teaching the child to self-monitor in the Social Standards program does not mean to hand the "student page" out and expect the student to follow its steps without telling her why it is important to follow certain rules. As with every skill area the child needs instruction before she can be expected to perform the skill.

Instruction can be done in several ways: Teacher language is important. Most students respond positively to language when it is framed in an attempt to help the child. When reviewing the steps with a particular student the teacher should be as supportive with her choice of words as she would be when trying to teach an academic concept. While we are certainly a multicultural society, students need to understand that there is a social code of public behavior that everyone needs to follow to be successful in public situations. This can be taught to students while still being sensitive about an individual child's background. Always avoid blaming the child for her deficiency.

One way to teach social behavior is to write your own social story for the student to accompany the self-monitoring story. Social stories are not just for children with autism but work well for primary children of all types. To write a social story follow the benchmarks and put them into sentences the student can understand. Each step is written on its own page with a digital picture of the child performing the step. This gives the student a visual cue about what she looks like when interacting appropriately. The social story needs to be read twice a day for a minimum of two weeks. When the child is reading the story, a discussion with the teacher or another adult should take place. A copy of the story must be sent home because the family needs to follow through on its reading over weekends. The social story helps the student understand classroom expectations better than if she had no visual cue.

A teacher may choose to use a role-play method of showing a student what each step looks like in action. The child must have sufficient practice with the skills in a small group before he is expected to do them on his own. Visually demonstrating the skills and designing the story to match his personal needs helps the child understand what is expected of him in certain situations. It also gives that child an opportunity to have input into the steps he needs to learn to achieve proficiency, giving him ownership from the start. Students will respond better to a guided means of learning social behavior than they do to point systems or disciplinary procedures.

No matter how a teacher chooses to teach self-monitoring skills it is important to use supportive language, not engage in circular arguments, and to allow students to have some input into their own story so that they begin to take responsibility at the very beginning — not another set of rules handed down by an adult.

Ultimately teaching a student to monitor her own behavior leads to less control and a greater chance that the child will accept responsibility for her own behavior.

(Reference: Kohn, Alfie PUNISHED by REWARDS, Houghton Mifflin Co., 1993, pg. 154)

student portfolios

The concept of student portfolios is not new. Many teachers who have used a Reading or Writing Workshop approach to teaching language arts have used portfolios as a mean to collect evidence that documents the work of each student and tracks progress throughout the year.

The definition of portfolios can range from a three-ring notebook to a large expandable file folder or a even CD where the child's work has been scanned into a computer and recorded on a disc.

Portfolios are not just limited to language arts. Creative classroom teachers have seen the value of using portfolios to document the work and progress of a student in all areas. Social skills are but one area in which documenting a student's growth can be helpful to the teacher, the family and the child.

Another value to keeping a portfolio of the child's social progress is to help support a child's growth or lack of it at an IEP conference. A common complaint from parents of children enrolled in special education programs is that at IEP conferences they are told their child is improving or not improving based upon teacher observation, but receive little documentation to support it. With an increased demand for children to pass standards and to have IEPs used for more than file storage, a social skill portfolio that has been used with the child during the year gives you a visual record of skills the child has learned. Families are more willing to support and reinforce their child's program when they understand what is being taught.

The most important reason for keeping a portfolio record is that it gives the student who is learning how to monitor her own behavior a visual means of assessing her strengths. The goal statements, benchmarks and daily self-monitoring sheets help the student concentrate on positive growth. She eventually becomes more involved in her own learning and discovers how to set goals and develop self-directed behaviors which leads to more peer acceptance and an increased comfort zone at school.

sample portfolio sequence

social skill domains

The 53 social skills taught in this guide are organized into six categories:

I. getting ready

II. transitions

III. classroom

IV. breaks and special events

V. anyplace

VI. peer relationships

☆ *three super social skills*

I. arriving at school

1. getting ready for school

2. walking to school

3. waiting for the bus

4. riding the bus

5. arriving by car

II. transitions

6. transition into the building

7. individual transitions

8. going to the IMC

9. being in specials

10. standing in line

11. transition into specials

12. group transition

13. going to the office

14. checking out of school

III. classroom

15. visitor to the classroom

16. one-on-one

17. large group activities

18. transitions in class

19. quiet time

20. small group activities

21. getting organized

22. class jobs

social skill domains

IV. breaks and special events

V. anyplace

VI. peer relationships

☆ *three super social skills*

one
getting ready
for school

skills

1. getting ready for school
2. walking to school
3. waiting for the bus
4. arriving by bus
5. arriving by car

getting ready for school
teacher guidelines

narrative

Although it could be argued that getting ready for school is more of an organizational problem than a social skill, for those children who come to school unprepared, learning can be more difficult. Sometimes these children are anxious about how they look, are hungry, or concerned about the homework that was left on the kitchen table. This skill should be taught to those who need it as a stepping stone to promote success in other skill areas at school. The aid of parents or guardians must be enlisted as needed to help monitor the morning routine.

objective

The student will follow a daily routine which includes grooming, eating a breakfast, and putting all school materials into a backpack before leaving for school.

benchmarks

1. S checks appearance in a mirror.

2. S eats breakfast.

3. S gathers school materials and puts them into a backpack.

4. S has proper outer clothing.

5. S says goodbye to family members.

problem checklist

Getting ready for school can be less chaotic if a daily routine is established. Each of the above skills can be broken down into smaller steps: i.e., clothes to wear may have to put out at night. A checklist developed for checking and packing up homework. Book bags and outer clothing might need to be placed in the same spot everyday.

Children who get up late may need to have a breakfast bar or other foodstuffs put into the backpack so that they will not be hungry when they enter the classroom.

teacher's script

Say, "You have a lot of things to remember when you're getting ready to go to school. Make sure you check yourself in the mirror to see if you look okay, eat a good breakfast, take all your homework and school supplies in your backpack and make sure you're dressed for the weather."

getting ready for school

learn to prepare for school

date _____

time _____

setting _____

teacher _____

period _____

student name _____

_____

self-talk story

Getting ready for school in the morning is hard for me. I am sleepy and cannot always find my homework. My teacher is unhappy with me when I leave my homework at home. I need to follow a plan for getting organized and being ready for school.

self-monitoring checklist

M	T	W	R	F	
☐	☐	☐	☐	☐	1. I check myself in the mirror.
☐	☐	☐	☐	☐	2. I eat breakfast.
☐	☐	☐	☐	☐	3. I get my homework.
☐	☐	☐	☐	☐	4. I get the right clothes for the weather.
☐	☐	☐	☐	☐	5. I say goodbye to my family.

my story

M	T	W	R	F	
☐	☐	☐	☐	☐	_____
☐	☐	☐	☐	☐	_____
☐	☐	☐	☐	☐	_____
☐	☐	☐	☐	☐	_____
☐	☐	☐	☐	☐	_____

walking to school
teacher guidelines

narrative

Walking to school can be a rewarding experience for children with strong social skills, but it can also be a difficult time for those who struggle in this area, since it largely takes place out of the realm of adult supervision. Students who walk to school need to learn the social skills of communicating with fellow students, friends and crossing guards as well as paying attention to safety issues. Talking to friends while also paying attention to signal lights and crossing guard instructions can make an enjoyable start to the school day.

objective

Will greet fellow students, friends and crossing guards appropriately while paying attention to the safety rules when walking to school.

Benchmarks

1. S will be observant of moving vehicles and other hazards.

2. S will use sidewalks, crosswalks, and obey signal lights as well as crossing guards.

3. S will greet friends along the way to school.

4. S will continue to walk without being distracted by friends or other obstacles.

5. S will avoid talking to strangers.

problem checklist

Walking to school with a group of friends can be enjoyable. Children need to be aware of potential hazards such as cars backing out of driveways or speeding on the road as well as construction sites. Other hazards can include a group of children who gather to harass those walking. Sometimes an alternative route might need to be discussed.

Safety issues such as using sidewalks have to be stressed. Younger children may benefit from walking and talking with an older group of students. Negotiating with parents about how to assist children who are not as aware of safety issues may be necessary.

Greeting and thanking a crossing guard or law enforcer is appropriate, even expected, but children need to be discouraged from becoming friendly with a person they do not know. Each one of these benchmarks can be broken into smaller segments to teach separately before a child would have to be accountable for the entire procedure.

Mastering how to greet friends and adults such as the crossing guard is a necessary social interaction for children who struggle with acknowledging other people.

teacher's script

Say, "Walking to school is fun and it's good exercise, but it's important to be careful for the sake of safety. You need to watch out for cars when you cross driveways or the street, and to be careful around construction sites. If a bully or a group of kids give you a hard time, you can change your route or tell an adult about it."

walking to school

student page

date _____

time _____

setting _____

teacher _____

period _____

student name _____

_____

being careful walking to school

self-talk story

I walk to school everyday. I need to remember to stay on the sidewalks, watch for people in front of me and greet my friends when I see them. I have to cross where the crossing guard is so that I can be safe. The crossing guard always smiles when I thank him. I try to get to school as quickly as I can so that I am not late.

self-monitoring checklist

M	T	W	R	F	
☐	☐	☐	☐	☐	1. I watch for moving cars.
☐	☐	☐	☐	☐	2. I use sidewalks, lights and crossing guards.
☐	☐	☐	☐	☐	3. I greet kids I know.
☐	☐	☐	☐	☐	4. I get to school before the bell rings.
☐	☐	☐	☐	☐	5. I avoid adults I don't know.

my story

M	T	W	R	F
☐	☐	☐	☐	☐
☐	☐	☐	☐	☐
☐	☐	☐	☐	☐
☐	☐	☐	☐	☐
☐	☐	☐	☐	☐

_____

_____

_____

_____

_____

three

waiting for the bus
teacher guidelines

narrative

Too often children arrive at school feeling angry or sad because of interactions that happened while waiting for the school bus. Often the pick-up location is unsupervised and conflicts can arise there. Some students come to school upset over something that happened waiting for the bus, while others have problems at this time of the day because they do not understand how to have appropriate conversations. Some can be impulsive and have problems standing still or knowing how to control an over-active nervous system, and their difficult start to the school day can present problems for the classroom teacher.

objective

The student will be able to wait for and board the school bus according to school rules.

benchmarks

1. Upon arriving at the bus stop, S will wait in the designated area.

2. S will verbally greet the children who are waiting there.*

3. S will greet children who come later as they arrive.*

4. S will interact, keeping to socially appropriate topics.

5. When the bus arrives, S will wait patiently to get on the bus without pushing or crowding the other children.

problem checklist

Students may need to practice how to greet other children. Some times it is appropriate to say, "Hi!" or nod one's head. If there is a group of children not willing to reciprocate the social greeting then learning how to maintain a prudent distance from the group, to avoid future conflicts may need to be a priority.

Teaching children how to begin a social conversation may need to be included in order for a child to learn the benchmarks which lead to the mastery of the objective. A conversation can start as simply as, "Hi (the person's name), did you see the football game on TV last night?"

Learning to line up and to wait without pushing or complaining is important in order to board the bus in an orderly fashion. Some children need to be taught how to do this because they have difficulty being crowded by others.

For children with a severe disability it could be beneficial to have a student friend to help model the rules for waiting for the bus. For really difficult situations the teacher may have to advocate having an adult supervisor to prevent problems from occurring. In rare situations an alternate pick-up stop may have to be assigned for the child having extreme difficulty.

teacher's script

Say, "It's fun to wait at the bus stop for your friends to take the bus to school together. When you arrive, greet the kids who are there and when others arrive, greet them too. Talk about appropriate things with the other students and try to avoid arguments. When the bus arrives, wait patiently to get on without pushing others."

30

waiting for the bus

student page

date _____

time _____

setting _____

teacher _____

period _____

student name _____

_____

waiting patiently for the bus

self-talk story

I would like to be able to wait patiently at the school bus stop and talk to the other kids who are waiting for a ride to school. I need to come up with a plan that will help me during this time so that I can get on the bus without having problems.

self-monitoring checklist

M	T	W	R	F	
☐	☐	☐	☐	☐	1. I find a place to wait.
☐	☐	☐	☐	☐	2. I say hi to kids there.
☐	☐	☐	☐	☐	3. I say hi to kids arriving.
☐	☐	☐	☐	☐	4. I talk about okay things.
☐	☐	☐	☐	☐	5. I wait patiently to board.

my story

M	T	W	R	F	
☐	☐	☐	☐	☐	_____
☐	☐	☐	☐	☐	_____
☐	☐	☐	☐	☐	_____
☐	☐	☐	☐	☐	_____
☐	☐	☐	☐	☐	_____

riding the bus

teacher guidelines

narrative

The ride on the school bus can provide many opportunities for children to act out and cause conflict. The driver has to spend most of his energy concentrating on the traffic and does not have the time or resources to mediate conflicts between children. This ride can set the tone for how the school day will proceed for individual students. Those who get off of the bus angry or defiant can change the mood of the entire classroom for that day. Teaching children how to monitor their own behavior in these unsupervised situations is not an easy task.

objective

The student will ride the bus each day and comply with the rules.

benchmarks

1. S will greet the bus driver after boarding the bus.

2. S will walk to a seat and sit down. (Will buckle a seat belt on buses that have them.)

3. S will remain in the bus seat until it stops at the school.

4. S will converse with other children using appropriate topics and voice volume.

5. After the bus arrives at school, S will check for belongings and walk off the bus respecting other children's body spaces.

problem checklist

In adult working situations, coworkers who ignore others are perceived as having poor social skills or as being just plain rude. It's no different with children. In order to develop appropriate social skills students need to practice them early and repeatedly. Teaching children to make a simple greeting of adults, such as the bus driver, encourages better social interactions. For children who are shy a simple smile and nod is an adequate starting point.

Bus rides can be long. Children who have difficulty sitting still may need to learn to read a book or listen with earphones to a CD player or squeeze a small ball in their pocket to keep from jumping up and down in the seat.

Some children may need to have an assigned seat or sit with an older child to help monitor themselves and to avoid excessive teasing.

In rare incidents while a child is learning the skills of riding a bus an adult may need to supervise.

For students who harass others or are being harassed a plan must be developed to help eliminate this behavior.

teacher's script

Say, "When you get on the bus, greet the driver with respect as you would any adult, and take your seat. If it has a seat belt, buckle in. You can have fun on the bus, but stay in your seat and talk in a normal voice. When you arrive at school, make sure you have all your things."

riding the bus

student page

riding
the bus

date _____

time _____

setting _____

teacher _____

period _____

student name _____

_____

self-talk story

I must get on the bus and ride it to school using rules which make it safe for everyone. I need to develop a plan and follow it so that I can ride to school safely.

self-monitoring checklist

M T W R F

1. I greet the bus driver with respect.
2. I sit down quietly.
3. I stay in my seat.
4. I talk to friends quietly.
5. I make sure I have my stuff.

my story

M T W R F

_____

_____

_____

_____

_____

arriving by car
teacher guidelines

narrative

Many parents drive their children to school, especially if the weather is too cold or it is raining hard. There are social rules for riding in a car as a passenger. Adherence to social rules links to safety rules. If a child is trying to switch radio stations or refuses to buckle a seat belt the driver's attention is distracted from watching the traffic.

objective

The student will ride in the car and observe the family rules for passengers.

benchmarks

1. S will sit in the seat assigned by the driver.

2. S will buckle the seat belt.

3. S will converse politely with the other people in the car.

4. S will avoid distracting the driver.

5. S will open the doors after the car has stopped and thank the driver.

problem checklist

For those children who do not have the social skills or don't wish to carry on an appropriate conversation, this time in the morning might be used to review math facts or spelling words. For the child who has difficulty starting conversations this can be a good time to practice initiating conversations such as "Hey mom, do we have plans for the weekend?"

Other children — who can be impulsive or demanding and can distract the driver by changing the radio stations or CD players, playing with the power windows or arguing — could use a plan to prevent these behaviors from occurring daily.

Sometimes it might be necessary to help the family negotiate the seating arrangement or radio station, or other appropriate adaptations to their routine.

teacher's script

Say, "When you ride to school with your parent or caregiver, or go with another family, it's important to be polite to the driver and not distract them from their driving. Most people don't like to sit in a car in silence, so if you can think of something to say the driver will appreciate it. When we arrive at school, thank the driver."

arriving by car

student page

date _____

time _____

setting _____

teacher _____

period _____

student name _____

_____

learning to ride in car

self-talk story

I like having a ride to school. I can use this time to practice what I have learned in school. But sitting for a long time in a car can be hard for me. I need to follow the rules and to thank the driver for bringing me to school.

self-monitoring checklist

M T W R F

1. I sit where I am told to sit.
2. I buckle my seat belt.
3. I talk about okay stuff.
4. I don't distract the driver.
5. I thank the driver.

my story

M T W R F

_____

_____

_____

_____

_____

two

transitions

skills

six

transition into the building
teacher guidelines

narrative
Coming into the school building from outside is hard for children because they have difficulty calming down after being stimulated by the noise and activity on school grounds. Other children may be angry because of a conflict and will bring it into the school. These children may need practice on this transition using established school rules. At the beginning of the year the entire class needs to review rules and procedures for entering the school building.

objective
When given the signal to enter the building the student will line up and walk quietly into the school.

benchmarks
1. When the signal to enter the building is heard, S will stop playing.
2. S will walk toward the building.
3. S will wait in line until given the direction to enter the building.
4. S will check shoes for grass, dirt, or snow and follow the rules for standing in line.
5. S will use the appropriate hallway voice after entering the building.

problem checklist
Some children have a hard time stopping an activity such as soccer or basketball when the signal to enter the school building is heard. They may have problems making such a transition smoothly. A modification may be that the student has to stop before a second or third warning. This would give these students an opportunity to start to regulate their own ability to make a transition.

There are always some children who run straight from the playground into the school, barely slowing along the way. Try helping them pick a landmark, such as the bike rack or a tree, where they begin walking so they can slow down before coming into the crowded school entrance.

Once inside the school some children have difficulty lowering their voices. Again, pick a landmark in the hallway that can serve as a visual cue to lower the voice. This will help them monitor their volume. Or arrange for the child who struggles with this to walk with a group of children who are able to control their voice volume.

Avoid having children who often have disputes on the playground take places in the middle of the line. It may work better to give them an assigned spot or to have them come in at a different time. Another approach would be to provide extra supervision to prevent them from bringing their anger into the classroom. They may also have to be assigned a quiet, supervised place to go to clam down and process their anger before returning to classroom.

teacher's script
Say, "When you're on the playground it's okay to run around and speak in a loud voice, but when you hear the bell, it's time to come into school. Then you have to slow down and speak more softly. When you're coming in the door and hanging up your coat, try not to bump into other kids. If you're feet are dirty, wipe them off before you enter the building."

transition into the building

student page

coming in to the school from the playground

date _____

time _____

setting _____

teacher _____

period _____

student name _____

_____

self-talk story

I like being outside but sometimes coming into the school building can be difficult. It's hard to slow down and to use a voice volume that is soft enough so I do not distract other classrooms. I like being with my friends and they like playing with me when I follow the rules.

self-monitoring checklist

M	T	W	R	F
☐	☐	☐	☐	☐
☐	☐	☐	☐	☐
☐	☐	☐	☐	☐
☐	☐	☐	☐	☐
☐	☐	☐	☐	☐

1. I stop playing when the bell rings.
2. I slow down and walk.
3. I stay in line until I go in.
4. I make sure my shoes are clean.
5. I use my inside school voice.

my story

M	T	W	R	F
☐	☐	☐	☐	☐
☐	☐	☐	☐	☐
☐	☐	☐	☐	☐
☐	☐	☐	☐	☐
☐	☐	☐	☐	☐

_____

_____

_____

_____

_____

individual transitions

teacher guidelines

narrative

In the modern classroom children are coming and going at all times. Speech classes, special reading classes, passes to the IMC or computer lab, and music lessons are but a few places that elementary students go in the course of a typical school day. Individual students who are leaving the classroom and transitioning by themselves need to master a certain protocol.

They must remember to take any school materials required when they leave. If they forget something, they must return to the class and retrieve it without disturbing the other students.

They must be able to walk the hallway without disturbing students in other classes.

They must go straight to their destination without making detours.

objective

When the student needs to leave the classroom for a destination, he/she will leave quietly and on time, taking all of the materials needed and walk directly there.

benchmarks

1. S will leave on time for the destination.
2. S will take all necessary materials before leaving the classroom.
3. S will walk out of the room quietly.
4. S will go directly to the destination.
5. S will greet adults and students in a friendly manner.

problem checklist

Once in the hallway some students can become distracted by friends, displays, or go to the bathrooms and stall for time. To eliminate this behavior a timed pass initially may need to be included.

For highly disorganized students the scheduled time and a checklist of what they need to take before leaving the classroom should be posted on their desk in an inconspicuous place.

For students with certain disabilities the name of the room/person that they need to go to can be carried with them to give to the adult when they arrive.

teacher's script

Say, "When you are by yourself in the hallway, it's easy to become distracted by displays or other students. Remember that you are in the hall because you are going somewhere and you need to get there and back as soon as possible."

individual transitions

student page

going places by myself

date _____

time _____

setting _____

teacher _____

period _____

student name _____

_____

self-talk story

At the right time I must remember to go. I need to take everything with me and not talk to my friends as I leave the classroom. I have to go directly there. If I see someone I know in the hallway, I can say hi to him or her but I must remember to keep walking. If I have everything I need and get there on time I feel ready to learn.

self-monitoring checklist

M	T	W	R	F
☐	☐	☐	☐	☐
☐	☐	☐	☐	☐
☐	☐	☐	☐	☐
☐	☐	☐	☐	☐
☐	☐	☐	☐	☐

1. I leave on time.
2. I bring what I need.
3. I leave class quietly.
4. I go straight to where I'm going.
5. I greet people softly.

my story

M	T	W	R	F
☐	☐	☐	☐	☐
☐	☐	☐	☐	☐
☐	☐	☐	☐	☐
☐	☐	☐	☐	☐
☐	☐	☐	☐	☐

_____

_____

_____

_____

_____

going to the IMC

teacher guidelines

narrative

The IMC can be the center of learning when students have to do research or checkout fun reading materials. Students can go with their classroom or on their own whenever they need a new book. The IMC is often a quiet place to study and the usual classroom noise or voices are not acceptable. In this room, children who do not make transitions from one environment to another well can have difficulty following the rules found in most school IMCs.

objective

When in the IMC the student will get required materials, use a quiet voice, work without distracting others and put materials back in the appropriate place.

benchmarks

1. S will be able to give the reason for coming to the IMC.

2. S will enter quietly and locate the required materials.

3. S will ask for help if needed from one of the IMC staff or teacher.

4. S will go quietly to designated work area and start working.

5. S will put away the materials used in the appropriate place and leave the IMC without distracting others.

problem checklist

The IMC often requires students to be quieter than they are in a classroom: Even though a class may be there to do a research project, often other children from different grade levels are checking out materials. Working in a large room with less of an opportunity for the teacher to supervise can pose problems for children who lack the ability to do assignments on their own. These students may take advantage of the situation and spend time talking or be unwilling to start work until they are assisted by an adult. Helping them to monitor their own behavior can lead them towards more independence.

teacher's script

Say, "You will often need to go to the IMC to work on special assignments. You should know what your assignment is and how to find the materials you need. If you don't, ask the IMC staff. The IMC is a place to be quiet and do your work. When you're done, put the materials where they belong."

going to the IMC

student page

date _____

time _____

setting _____

teacher _____

period _____

student name _____

_____

self-talk story

During some of my classes I will go to the IMC to do research work. I must remember to enter the IMC quietly because I can not distract the students already there. I will go where I can get materials I need, but if I can't find it I will ask the IMC staff for help. When I get the books I need, I will sit down and start working. I must remember to be quiet and raise my hand if I need help. When I leave, I put the books back where they belong and line up without talking.

self-monitoring checklist

M	T	W	R	F	
☐	☐	☐	☐	☐	1. I know why I'm going to the IMC.
☐	☐	☐	☐	☐	2. I enter quietly and get materials.
☐	☐	☐	☐	☐	3. If needed, I ask for help.
☐	☐	☐	☐	☐	4. I take books to the work area.
☐	☐	☐	☐	☐	5. I put books back and return to class.

my story

M	T	W	R	F	
☐	☐	☐	☐	☐	_____
☐	☐	☐	☐	☐	_____
☐	☐	☐	☐	☐	_____
☐	☐	☐	☐	☐	_____
☐	☐	☐	☐	☐	_____

being in specials
teacher guidelines

narrative

Specials are part of the daily student routine, but since the teachers do not teach these classes every day they have a different relationship with the students than the regular classroom instructor. The structure in special classes is often more relaxed: e.g., PE classes, which are noisier and faster paced. A change in classroom structure or teacher can present problems for some children.

objective

When in the special classroom the student will greet the teacher and follow the class rules for that subject.

benchmarks

1. S will greet the teacher and go to assigned area.

2. S will listen and follow teacher directions.

3. S will get out all required materials/equipment.

4. S will raise hand when a question arises or needs to make a comment.

5. S will clean area and stand quietly in line until dismissed from the class.

problem checklist

Because they are not everyday classroom instructors, specials' teachers may need to be informed about students who have special needs, such as writing problems or those who don't like to be called upon in a large group situation. They should also be aware of children who have disabilities which could interfere with their performance (e.g., physical challenges in PE, or fine motor in art).

teacher's script

Say, "Specials are fun and offer you a change from classes like math and language arts, but they have rules, too. When you arrive, you need to greet your teacher, go to your assigned area, have your materials handy, listen to directions and clean up after yourself when class is over. Your specials teacher will appreciate your efforts in observing the rules."

being in specials
student page

date _____

time _____

setting _____

teacher _____

period _____

student name _____

_____

going to specials

self-talk story

When I am in a specials class, I will greet the teacher with respect. I will go to the place that I'm supposed to be and wait for the teacher's directions. I listen carefully to the teacher and I get out everything I need for today's lesson. I can raise my hand if I have a question. When the class is over I put away all the things I used. I wait in line for the teacher to tell us we can go back to class.

self-monitoring checklist

M	T	W	R	F	
☐	☐	☐	☐	☐	1. I say hi to my teacher and sit down.
☐	☐	☐	☐	☐	2. I look at teacher and listen.
☐	☐	☐	☐	☐	3. I get out what I need.
☐	☐	☐	☐	☐	4. I raise my hand to ask questions.
☐	☐	☐	☐	☐	5. I put things away and get in line.

my story

M	T	W	R	F	
☐	☐	☐	☐	☐	_____
☐	☐	☐	☐	☐	_____
☐	☐	☐	☐	☐	_____
☐	☐	☐	☐	☐	_____
☐	☐	☐	☐	☐	_____

standing in line
teacher guidelines

narrative

Students are constantly required to stand in line for one reason or another. This can be difficult for some and predispose them to inappropriate behaviors. For example, if the class must wait outside of a specials class, some students may take advantage of the teacher standing with her back to the line waiting for students to enter the lab. It can be a tempting time for some kids to become verbally or physically abusive to peers.

Other students who are impatient or have limited attention spans don't like to wait in a lunch line and will butt in to get served first.

Still others have body space issues and are unable to tolerate standing with people on either side of them.

Chatty students may find this an opportunity to carry on a social conversation. Loud students can interrupt teaching in other classrooms as they stand in the hallway.

Learning how to manage one's behavior while in line is essential because it happens so often throughout the school day. Standing in line also occurs in a community setting such as the grocery store or waiting to purchase movies tickets.

Review the rules for lining up and waiting in line at the beginning of the year. Reviewing social rules early for the whole class may prevent future problems.

Don't allow students to swap or change places in line once their place has been established.

objective

The student will stay in place in line, keeping hands to self and using acceptable school language.

benchmarks

1. S will stay in assigned (or established) spot.

2. S will stand with hands and feet to self.

3. S will be patient and move ahead with the line.

4. S will use voice volume cued by the teacher.

5. S will talk in acceptable school language.

problem checklist

Students who have trouble standing in line (e.g., a cafeteria line), or who have body space issues (e.g., a student with a severe attention deficit disorder) often act out when the line moves slowly. These students can manage their time better if they have a structured sequence of behaviors expected of them while standing and waiting in a crowded line.

teacher's script

Say, "Standing in line takes a lot of patience, but it's something you have to do a lot when you're in school, so you might as well get used to it. Once you have a place in line, stay there, keep your hands to yourself, move ahead as the line moves and don't talk too loud."

standing in line

student page

date _____

time _____

setting _____

teacher _____

period _____

student name _____

_____

self-talk story

When I am waiting in the line to get lunch I need to remember to stay in my own place. I have to respect other students and not let a friend cut in front of me. I have to try to keep my hands and feet to myself and not put them on the walls or lean against someone else. It is hard but I have to try to be patient and not get upset with those people in front of me because the line is moving slowly. I can talk to my friends in a normal classroom voice. We can talk about what we want to do at recess or make plans to do something together on the weekend.

self-monitoring checklist

M	T	W	R	F
☐	☐	☐	☐	☐
☐	☐	☐	☐	☐
☐	☐	☐	☐	☐
☐	☐	☐	☐	☐
☐	☐	☐	☐	☐

1. I stay in my place.
2. I keep hands to myself.
3. I am patient while I stand in line.
4. I talk in a normal voice.
5. I talk about okay things.

my story

M	T	W	R	F
☐	☐	☐	☐	☐
☐	☐	☐	☐	☐
☐	☐	☐	☐	☐
☐	☐	☐	☐	☐
☐	☐	☐	☐	☐

_____

_____

_____

_____

_____

transition into specials
teacher guidelines

narrative
Attending classes such as art, music, physical education or computer lab is a daily routine for most children in the elementary school. If the student enters these classes calm and ready to learn, it is helpful for the teacher and allows the child to experience success immediately. For children who have difficulty making transitions or managing their behavior, learning a procedure may prevent additional problems.

objective
When entering a special class the student will go to an assigned area and wait for teacher directions.

benchmarks
1. S will remain in line until the previous class exits.

2. S will enter quietly, keeping hands to self.

3. S will go to designated area.

4. S will look at the teacher and wait quietly for teacher directions.

5. S will listen to the instructor's directions and raise hand for questions.

problem checklist
Some students have difficulty entering a room such as the computer lab and feel compelled to touch the equipment as they go to their assigned area. The second benchmark needs to be stressed in this situation.

Some students have trouble with the noise level in a large classroom such as the gym. These children may need to have a visual marker where they can place themselves and help screen out the noise level. Having a partner to help may also prepare them for listening to the teacher.

teacher's script
Say, "Even though you don't go to specials everyday, like math or English, you still need to mind the rules. When you're in hallway, waiting to come into a specials class, let the other class leave first. Enter quietly, keeping your hands to yourself and go to your place in the class. Listen carefully to and obey the teacher's instructions. If you follow these rules, you'll enjoy most specials and the teachers will enjoy you."

transition into specials

student page

coming into specials from the hallway	date _____
	time _____
	setting _____
	teacher _____
	period _____
	student name _____
	_____

self-talk story

My special classes are fun, but sometimes I have trouble getting ready to listen. I need to walk quietly into the classroom and to wait for teacher directions before I start an activity or use the materials in the class.

self-monitoring checklist

M T W R F

□ □ □ □ □   1. I stay outside until class leaves.
□ □ □ □ □   2. I walk in keeping hands to myself.
□ □ □ □ □   3. I go to my seat.
□ □ □ □ □   4. I wait quietly for directions.
□ □ □ □ □   5. I listen and raise hand for help.

my story

M T W R F

□ □ □ □ □   _____
□ □ □ □ □   _____
□ □ □ □ □   _____
□ □ □ □ □   _____
□ □ □ □ □   _____

group transition
teacher guidelines

narrative

A significant part of every school day is group transitioning from grade level classrooms to another class in the building. This can be a problem for students who struggle with managing behavior or who feel uncomfortable surrounded by other children. However, an orderly and quiet transition, when in the hallway, is important so students in other classes are not disturbed.

Because of potential consequences, you may want to start using this guide at the beginning of the year to insure that all students know to learn how to behave when making a large group transition from classroom to another part of the building.

An individual child may need to practice this behavior and the student page self-monitoring checklist can be used as a way for that child to monitor her own behavior.

objective

When given the verbal cue to line up and walk to another part of the building, the student will be able to follow the school rules for behavior during a large group transition.

benchmarks

1. S will stand up and walk to designated spot in the line.
2. S will bring all required materials, stand quietly in line and look at the teacher.
3. S will walk using the rule for voices and appropriate space when in the hallway.
4. S will walk in the hallway with hands to her side.
5. S will stay in order and wait quietly at the door of a special class or other large group activity until the teacher gives directions.

problem checklist

Although children make many group trips from the classroom to a special, or to the cafeteria or assembly, some still need extra instruction on their behaviors while transitioning — just as if they had to learn a math or grammatical concept.

Children who have behavior problems that interfere with their learning may need extra guided practice to learn this skill.

Children with autism may initially have to be in a certain spot in the line or stand next to someone who makes them feel comfortable.

Some children may not understand nonverbal social cues and have to be taught to read body gestures as well as how to make a transition.

Some children need to learn the social language for a group situation such as "excuse me" if they accidentally bump into another person.

teacher's script

Say, "Often you have to walk with your whole class to another part of the building. You have to go to art, or music or assembly or other places. When you do, it's important to listen to your teacher and be quiet so you don't disturb other children in their classes. If your teacher asks you to walk in a long, straight line, you should obey her. That makes your teacher and your classmates happy."

group transition
student page

date _____

time _____

setting _____

teacher _____

period _____

student name _____

_____

walking together with your class

self-talk story

I often have to walk with my class to another part of the school for art, music, PE or assembly. When I have to walk the halls in a large group, my teachers and classmates expect me to walk in a long line and to behave myself. I need to be quiet so I don't disturb kids in other classes. When I follow the school rules it pleases my teacher and other students will enjoy walking with me in the hallway.

self-monitoring checklist

M T W R F

1. I line up and wait for directions.
2. I bring materials I need.
3. I am aware of my voice volume and my body space.
4. I keep hands to myself.
5. I stay in order until we arrive.

my story

M T W R F

_____
_____
_____
_____
_____

thirteen
going to the office
teacher guidelines

narrative

Children often leave the classroom to go to other parts of the school building such as the IMC, the guidance counselor's room or the general school office. When the student is sent to the school office he needs to understand that he is a representative of the class and how he behaves reflects his classroom and his teacher as well as how other adults view him. Children who are messengers to the offices as part of the classroom jobs need to know how to behave and how to follow a schedule.

objective

When given the direction to go to the school office the student will walk to and from there and interact appropriately with office personal.

benchmarks

1. S will follow the schedule for going to the office when assigned the job.

2. S will walk directly to the office.

3. S will wait patiently until one of the office staff acknowledges him/her.

4. S will greet the secretary (or other staff) appropriately and thank her for helping.

5. S will return directly to the classroom.

problem checklist

Initially, some children may need to have a friend go with them when running an errand outside of the classroom. Children who perform this skill correctly should be praised. "Joey, Mrs. Brown said you were very polite when you came to the office this morning. She was impressed with the way you asked for help." Giving specific praise about a behavior can teach a child what it was he did well.

The behavior of students from a given class, when they're in the office, creates an indelible impression about how capable its teacher is and whether or not her students are under control. It's an issue most veteran teachers are acutely aware of and new teachers will soon come to realize.

teacher's script

Say, "When you go the office you are a representative of your class, so it's important that you are on your best behavior. Go there directly, be polite to the office staff and return directly. When you do these things, your teacher and other students will be pleased with you."

going to the office

student page

date _____

time _____

setting _____

teacher _____

period _____

student name _____

_____

self-talk story

When it is my turn to be office messenger I need to walk directly to the office. If the secretary is busy, I must wait quietly until she can help me. I can say, "Excuse me, I need your help." I have to thank the office staff for helping and come directly back to my classroom.

self-monitoring checklist

M	T	W	R	F
☐	☐	☐	☐	☐
☐	☐	☐	☐	☐
☐	☐	☐	☐	☐
☐	☐	☐	☐	☐
☐	☐	☐	☐	☐

1. I go to the office if asked.
2. I walk directly there.
3. I wait calmly for secretary.
4. I greet her and say what I need.
5. I thank her and return to class.

my story

M	T	W	R	F
☐	☐	☐	☐	☐
☐	☐	☐	☐	☐
☐	☐	☐	☐	☐
☐	☐	☐	☐	☐
☐	☐	☐	☐	☐

_____

_____

_____

_____

_____

checking out of school

teacher guidelines

narrative

Students who leave their homework at school or forget to bring important notes home are predisposed to start the next school day stressed. They may be despondent because they do not have an assignment completed or neglect to take home field trip notices or other important announcements to their family.

Often children leave in such a rush they forget to take personal items with them. If the child is unable to find his things the next day, it can create a stressful feeling that will permeate his school day. Getting students to follow a consistent checkout routine is important for those who may have difficulty organizing themselves.

objective

At the end of the school day the student will check for all homework assignments and notes, take all personal items, and walk to the designated transportation area.

benchmarks

1. S will check to see all homework and notes are in the take-home folder.

2. S will walk quietly out of the classroom after being dismissed by the teacher.

3. S will stop at the locker, put the take-home folder into a backpack and gather personal items to take home.

4. S will walk and talk in an orderly manner in the hallways.

5. S will go directly to the bus or other area to go home.

problem checklist

For students who have trouble organizing homework, provide a checklist or assignment sheet so they can be sure that everything that has to be taken home is in their homework folder. Getting children to be responsible for this is important because it alleviates future problems that can occur when homework is not finished.

Once outside the classroom, students need to double check that they have all of their personal items such as coats, hats, mittens and anything else they may have brought to school that day.

teacher's script

Say, "It's important to remember to take your things home at the end of the school day. If you forget something, like your homework, it puts you behind in your school work and makes your teachers disappointed. If you forget something like gloves or a computer game, they might not be there the next day."

checking out of school

student page

remembering your things at the end of the school day

date _____

time _____

setting _____

teacher _____

period _____

student name _____

_____

self-talk story

At the end of the day I check that all of the notes home and my homework are in my take-home folder. I wait until my teacher dismisses me and walk to my locker. I put my take-home folder into the backpack and put on my jacket. I check that I haven't forgotten anything.

self-monitoring checklist

M	T	W	R	F
☐	☐	☐	☐	☐
☐	☐	☐	☐	☐
☐	☐	☐	☐	☐
☐	☐	☐	☐	☐
☐	☐	☐	☐	☐

1. I get my homework and my belongings.
2. I wait until I am dismissed.
3. I stop at cubby and make sure I have everything.
4. I leave the school quietly.
5. I wait for bus or ride.

my story

M	T	W	R	F
☐	☐	☐	☐	☐
☐	☐	☐	☐	☐
☐	☐	☐	☐	☐
☐	☐	☐	☐	☐
☐	☐	☐	☐	☐

_____

_____

_____

_____

_____

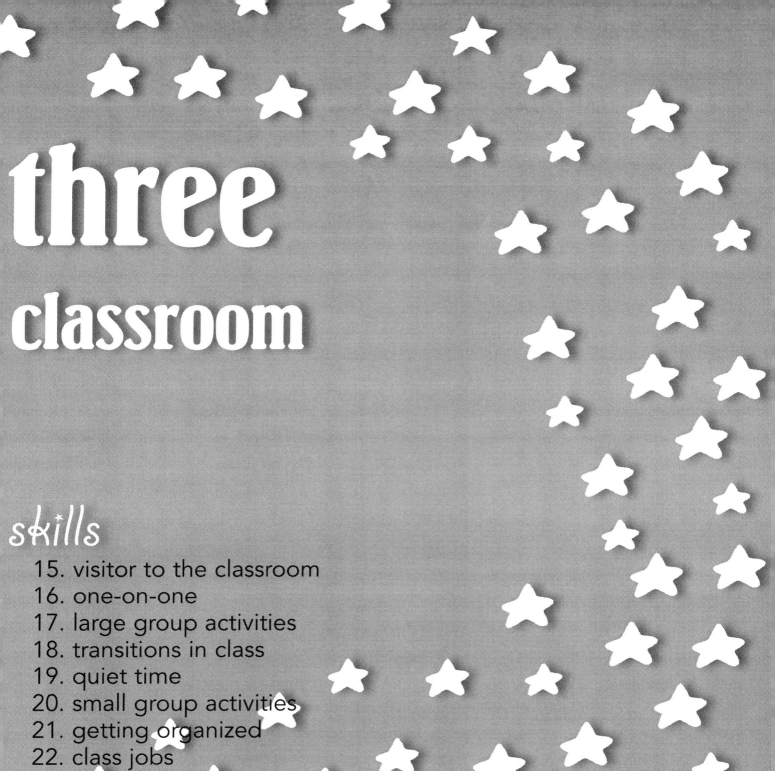

three

classroom

skills

fifteen
visitor to the classroom
teacher guidelines

narrative

It is not uncommon for visitors to frequent classrooms for a variety of reasons: Parent or student volunteers, guidance counselors, parents who want to share information about a trip they may have taken, or an expert on a subject the class has been studying. All these can enhance a learning situation. Because it changes the normal dynamics, children need to know how to interact when a visitor is in a classroom. Some students will struggle with this more than others and they will need a little extra instruction.

objective

When a visitor comes to the classroom the student will greet him or her, listen and participate in the discussion and thank the visitor for coming.

benchmarks

1. S will greet the visitor.

2. S will recognize the purpose of the visit.

3. S will not stare at the visitor.

4. S will listen and participate according to the purpose of the visit.

5. S will thank the visitor for coming.

problem checklist

Some visitors, such as a parent/student volunteer, may have a regularly scheduled time to come to the class. They generally work with a small number of children. The activity of the volunteer and the group of children who are working with him may distract those students who do not work with him. A new person in the room may be especially distracting for children with autism. Learning how to handle this intrusion and to continue working is important for the rhythm of the class environment and that student's educational program. Teaching the social rules for accepting visitors is important for these students.

Other children may not see a visitor as someone who deserves the same respect as the teacher. Just as the child with a disability needs it, these students need to be taught the social rules for including the visitor in the classroom routine.

Foreshadowing expectations of student behavior before the visitor arrives can be helpful.

teacher's script

Say, "Sometimes visitors come to your classroom. Some might be volunteers who work with certain students and others might be there to talk to the class. You should greet and treat them with respect like you would any adult and listen carefully if they make a presentation. When they're done, you should thank them. Your teacher will appreciate your good behavior."

visitor to the classroom

student page

date _____

time _____

setting _____

teacher _____

period _____

student name _____

_____

self-talk story

Sometimes visitors come to class to help my teacher. They come for different reasons. Some are there to help students with a lesson. They can even be parents of other students. Others come to talk to my class about interesting things they know a lot about. I can greet them with respect and listen carefully to what they have to say. If the visitor is helping other students, I must remember to continue doing my own work. When the visitors help me, or speak to the class I will thank them.

self-monitoring checklist

M	T	W	R	F
☐	☐	☐	☐	☐
☐	☐	☐	☐	☐
☐	☐	☐	☐	☐
☐	☐	☐	☐	☐
☐	☐	☐	☐	☐

1. I greet class visitors politely.
2. I know why the visitor is here.
3. I don't stare at or bother visitor.
4. I listen carefully to visitor.
5. I thank the visitor for coming.

my story

M	T	W	R	F
☐	☐	☐	☐	☐
☐	☐	☐	☐	☐
☐	☐	☐	☐	☐
☐	☐	☐	☐	☐
☐	☐	☐	☐	☐

_____
_____
_____
_____

one-on-one

teacher guidelines

narrative

Individual students who need extra help often have opportunities to work in a one-on-one teaching situation. Parent/student volunteers, educational assistants, and teachers are some of the one-on-one options available. Many students enjoy the additional attention and feel more comfortable than in a larger setting. For some, it's an invaluable aid for keeping up with their classmates.

Other students find this teaching approach difficult to manage. A withdrawn child or one who has a very poor trust level may not be comfortable until they have had an opportunity to practice the rules for a one-on-one approach.

objective

When given a one-on-one teaching situation the student will listen to and follow the directions, ask questions and complete work.

benchmarks

1. S will bring all materials to the instructor.

2. S will look at and listen to the instructor.

3. S will ask questions and follow directions.

4. S will begin work immediately and stay on task.

5. S will thank the instructor for helping.

problem checklist

For children who have certain disabilities or whose trust level is poor, it may help to foreshadow the event before they actually begin to work in a one-on-one situation, especially if the person is not the classroom teacher. Checking in with the student during the one-on-one time may also alleviate some uncertainties on the part of the student.

teacher's script

Say, "Sometimes you might need some extra help. Working one-on-one with a teacher, an aide or a volunteer can help you a lot to get caught up on your work. When you work one-on-one it's important to bring your materials, pay attention, follow directions and stay on task. When you're finished, don't forget to say thank you."

one-on-one
student page

date _____

time _____

setting _____

teacher _____

period _____

student name _____

_____

working one-on-one

self-talk story

My teacher told me that I will be working one-on-one. I must remember to bring everything. I must look at and listen to my instructor so that I can understand what to do. If I have questions, I can ask. This is a time to work hard and get my assignment finished. When it's over, I will thank him for helping me.

self-monitoring checklist

M	T	W	R	F
☐	☐	☐	☐	☐
☐	☐	☐	☐	☐
☐	☐	☐	☐	☐
☐	☐	☐	☐	☐
☐	☐	☐	☐	☐

1. I bring everything I need.
2. I look at and listen to teacher.
3. I follow directions.
4. I begin my work and try to finish.
5. I thank the person for help.

my story

M	T	W	R	F
☐	☐	☐	☐	☐
☐	☐	☐	☐	☐
☐	☐	☐	☐	☐
☐	☐	☐	☐	☐
☐	☐	☐	☐	☐

_____

_____

_____

_____

_____

large group activities
teacher guidelines

narrative

Much of the school day is spent teaching and learning in a large group. Some children use this as an opportunity to socialize with a friend because the teacher's attention is on the entire class rather than on individual students. Other children may be paying attention but do not observe the rules for gaining teacher attention. Instead they will talk out or ask questions without raising their hand. Interruptions can affect the flow of a lesson and these children have to be taught how to participate without disturbing others. At the beginning of the year the entire class will benefit from reviewing the social rules for listening in a large group situation.

objective

When in a large group activity the student will listen, follow teacher directions and raise her hand to ask questions or make comments.

benchmarks

1. S will look at the teacher and sit quietly while she is speaking.

2. S will begin working at the teacher's request.

3. S will use other students as models to cue work

4. S will raise hand to ask questions or make comments.

5. S will stay on task until the group goal is achieved.

problem checklist

While it's appropriate for students to talk out loud about the lesson or classroom procedures (and it shows they are paying attention), some may need to be cued to first raise their hand. Once the instructor has made the student aware of this, he should make an effort to call on the student when she does raise her hand appropriately. That should help reduce the spontaneous, but well-intentioned talking out.

When teaching in a large group situation, make a point of praising those children who are listening appropriately. These students will then serve as a model for others.

teacher's script

Say, "When the whole class is working together on a project it's important to pay close attention to what the teacher says and to cooperate with other members of your class to get the assignment done. When everyone works together and does a good job, it makes the whole class and the teacher feel good."

large group activities

student page

date _____

time _____

setting _____

teacher _____

period _____

student name _____

_____

large group activities

self-talk story

The teacher is talking and I need to remember to sit quietly and listen. When she tells the class to begin working I need to start my own work. If I forget what I'm supposed to do I can look at the other students. If I still need help I can raise my hand. When I say something during class time I need to talk about what the teacher is teaching.

self-monitoring checklist

M	T	W	R	F	
☐	☐	☐	☐	☐	1. I sit quietly and pay attention.
☐	☐	☐	☐	☐	2. I start my work.
☐	☐	☐	☐	☐	3. I watch others for what to do.
☐	☐	☐	☐	☐	4. I raise hand for questions.
☐	☐	☐	☐	☐	5. I pay attention to my work until I'm finished.

my story

M	T	W	R	F	
☐	☐	☐	☐	☐	_____
☐	☐	☐	☐	☐	_____
☐	☐	☐	☐	☐	_____
☐	☐	☐	☐	☐	_____
☐	☐	☐	☐	☐	_____

transitions in class

teacher guidelines

narrative

Throughout the school day the class is asked to make constant transitions. When these aren't well controlled, it can result in a chaotic and noisy time. Some students take it as an opportunity to socialize and this can waste important instructional time when the teacher is trying to initiate a new learning activity.

In-class transitions also offer an opportunity for the teacher to assess which children are more independent in their ability to listen to and follow teacher directions. This can give you clues early in the year as to which students you will want to concentrate on with this program.

objective

When given teacher direction to start an activity the student will be able to comply.

benchmarks

1. S will look at the teacher and listen quietly to her instructions.

2. S will gather all materials necessary to complete the task.

3. S will sit quietly at her desk or move quietly to the assigned area.

4. S will raise her hand if she has a question about the assignment.

5. When given the direction to begin, S will start the assignment.

problem checklist

Some students may not be able to look at the teacher because of a disability (e.g., a child with autism). Teachers should double check to insure that these students have heard the directions.

Some children have poor attention spans and may need to be taught how to cue into classmate behaviors so they can model and start the assignment with less confusion about what they need to do.

Some children may need to have a silent signal to get teacher help because they feel uncomfortable asking questions in a large group.

teacher's script

Say, "Every time your class changes subjects, like from math to language arts, you need to get your materials ready, make sure you're in the right place in the classroom and be as quiet as you can. If you have any questions, raise your hand and listen to your teacher's directions to start working."

transitions in class

student page

date _____

time _____

setting _____

teacher _____

period _____

student name _____

_____

changing subjects

self-talk story

The teacher often asks me to start a new assignment. Sometimes I will need to stay at my desk. Other times I will need to move to another part of the room. It is important that I pay attention to what the teacher tells the class so that I have the right materials and I can start an assignment according to the directions.

self-monitoring checklist

M	T	W	R	F	
☐	☐	☐	☐	☐	1. I look at and listen to teacher.
☐	☐	☐	☐	☐	2. I get materials for new subject.
☐	☐	☐	☐	☐	3. I stay or move to new area.
☐	☐	☐	☐	☐	4. I raise my hand for questions.
☐	☐	☐	☐	☐	5. I start when the teacher says.

my story

M	T	W	R	F
☐	☐	☐	☐	☐
☐	☐	☐	☐	☐
☐	☐	☐	☐	☐
☐	☐	☐	☐	☐
☐	☐	☐	☐	☐

_____

_____

_____

_____

_____

nineteen

quiet time

teacher guidelines

narrative

Throughout the day there are periods when it benefits the class as a whole to have quiet breaks such as silent reading time, taking a test or quiz, or finishing a written assignment. On occasion there are a few students who really struggle with being quiet during these periods and may need some extra help managing their noise and activity levels. Some students, especially those who are inclined to be socially active, would rather talk to each other than be quietly focused on their work. Quiet time actually benefits these students by asking them to observe the discipline of silence.

objective

When given teacher direction that quiet time has begun, the student will sit and work on the required assignment without distracting others.

benchmarks

1. S remains in assigned area throughout the quiet period.

2. S works on the assigned task.

3. S pays attention to the task until finished or is given the direction to stop working.

4. If the assignment is finished, S will do other acceptable tasks.

5. S will remain quiet and raise hand before making a comment or asking question.

problem checklist

As mentioned, making the transition to a quiet time is difficult for some students. These children may need to have a list of acceptable tasks to do during quiet time. A posted list in the classroom can also serve as a reference to all students.

teacher's script

Say, "Quiet times give you a chance to catch up on homework, read books or other tasks. It's important for you to stay in your place in class during this time and to do your assigned work. If the quiet time is for reading, make sure you have something to read."

quiet time
student page

date _____

time _____

setting _____

teacher _____

period _____

student name _____

_____

quiet time

self-talk story

The teacher just said that it is quiet work time. I need to do the task that was assigned. I need to sit without disturbing other children, which means I need to be quiet and stay in my own seat. If I have a question or comment I need to raise my hand and wait for the teacher to call on me.

M	T	W	R	F
☐	☐	☐	☐	☐
☐	☐	☐	☐	☐
☐	☐	☐	☐	☐
☐	☐	☐	☐	☐
☐	☐	☐	☐	☐

self-monitoring checklist

1. I stay quietly in place.
2. I follow directions.
3. I pay attention to work.
4. If I finish I can read or do homework.
5. I raise my hand for questions.

M	T	W	R	F
☐	☐	☐	☐	☐
☐	☐	☐	☐	☐
☐	☐	☐	☐	☐
☐	☐	☐	☐	☐
☐	☐	☐	☐	☐

my story

_____

_____

_____

_____

_____

small group activities
teacher guidelines

narrative

Cooperative groups or partner activities can contribute to learning as long as the group understands the work being done and the social rules for doing it. While it is hard for some children to share ideas or materials, others have problems functioning in a less structured situation. Children need to follow not only the rules for getting the work completed but also the social rules for conversation with others. The students need to talk with each other and ask for help from each other in an appropriate fashion.

objective

When working in small groups the student will make self-initiated attempts to do the assigned job, share materials, ideas and follow all social rules for interacting with the other students.

benchmarks

1. S will do the assigned job to help the group finish the assignment.

2. S will share materials when appropriate.

3. S will share at least one idea.

4. S will remember to thank members of the group who help.

5. S will compliment others on their work or ideas.

problem checklist

Some children find it difficult to work in small groups because they do not understand how to interact with other children in a way that allows the group to be productive. Children with poor social skills can sometimes function better if they are placed with more socially appropriate children rather than by placing them based on their academic abilities.

Some children have problems sharing and may need to have the steps for sharing materials broken down for them before they can learn to share and participate in a group. For example, a child might need to learn that if he shares, others might be more willing to help him by sharing as well. Sharing can help the other children enjoy having that child in the group.

Learning simple please and thank you statements can contribute to a more positive learning atmosphere.

teacher's script

Say, "In small group activities everyone must contribute to help the group succeed in finishing its job. Sometimes you have to share materials with other students and to help the group with your good ideas. When you do a good job, compliment others on their work and thank them all for working hard."

small group activities

student page

date _____

time _____

setting _____

teacher _____

period _____

student name _____

_____

small group activities

self-talk story

When I work with a partner or in a group I must remember to do my job. I need to think of one idea about how to help finish the assignment. I will share pencils, markers, books and other material with the group. I will remember to thank people for helping. I will give at least one put-up compliment to the group.

self-monitoring checklist

M	T	W	R	F	
☐	☐	☐	☐	☐	1. I do assigned job.
☐	☐	☐	☐	☐	2. I share materials.
☐	☐	☐	☐	☐	3. I share ideas.
☐	☐	☐	☐	☐	4. I thank those who helped.
☐	☐	☐	☐	☐	5. I compliment group members.

my story

M	T	W	R	F
☐	☐	☐	☐	☐
☐	☐	☐	☐	☐
☐	☐	☐	☐	☐
☐	☐	☐	☐	☐
☐	☐	☐	☐	☐

_____

_____

_____

_____

_____

getting organized

teacher guidelines

narrative

Making the transition from home to school can be difficult for some students. Going from a less structured environment to one which is fairly formal is a problem for children who struggle with such dramatic changes. For other students who have trouble getting organized, problems with this initial transition can affect their entire day, because they're starting off behind.

objective

The student will bring all homework and other school materials into the classroom and be seated and ready to learn by the final bell.

benchmarks

1. S will check book bag or cubby for homework and other materials.

2. S will bring required items into the classroom.

3. As S walks to the assigned seat, he/she will greet teacher and friends.

4. S will walk to the desk respecting other student's body space.

5. S will sit down and wait for teacher directions.

problem checklist

Some students seem to be always moving at a pace faster than necessary. When they are in a crowded situation such as lines or aisles in the classroom they often bump into other children. These students may simply need to be taught how to enter a room and what words to use when they accidentally bump into another child.

Very shy children can be taught to smile at their peers rather than rushing by and ignoring them.

It's a good idea to check and see if students who struggle with organizational skills have all required items to begin their school day. Going through this with them a few times is usually all that's needed. This gives them a greater sense of readiness and won't interrupt your class so much for constant returns to retrieve something forgotten from their book bag or cubby.

teacher's script

Say, "When the school day begins, you should be organized and ready for your first class. Before you go in the classroom make sure you have the materials you need from your book bag or cubby. Go to your assigned seat, greet your friends and teacher and sit down and wait for the teacher's directions. If you do these things, it will be a good start for your school day."

getting organized

student page

getting
organized

date _____

time _____

setting _____

teacher _____

period _____

student name _____

_____

self-talk story

Starting the school day smoothly will help me learn better. I need to check my book bag (or cubby) for all of the things I need to bring into the class. I have to remember to walk so that I do not bump into another student in the classroom. I can greet my friends by smiling or saying "hi". I have to sit down and wait for my teacher's directions. I can talk in a normal voice until the bell rings then I have to be quiet.

self-monitoring checklist

M	T	W	R	F
☐	☐	☐	☐	☐
☐	☐	☐	☐	☐
☐	☐	☐	☐	☐
☐	☐	☐	☐	☐
☐	☐	☐	☐	☐

1. I get materials from bag and cubby.
2. I check materials before class starts.
3. I talk quietly as I enter.
4. I am aware of other's space.
5. I sit quietly until bell rings.

my story

M	T	W	R	F
☐	☐	☐	☐	☐
☐	☐	☐	☐	☐
☐	☐	☐	☐	☐
☐	☐	☐	☐	☐
☐	☐	☐	☐	☐

_____

_____

_____

_____

_____

class jobs

teacher guidelines

narrative

Many children like to have the responsibility of a class job. Giving students a daily/weekly job helps to contribute to a classroom community of cooperation.

objective

When given a classroom job the student will complete the job without prompting.

benchmarks

1. S will learn how to do the job.

2. S will perform the job willingly.

3. S will stay on task until the job is completed.

4. S will be a good representative of her class when the job needs to be performed outside of the classroom (e.g., messenger to the office).

5. S will ask the teacher how to do the job if he forgets.

problem checklist

Students with a disability also need to participate and be as independent as possible in order to complete a classroom job. Giving these children a simple job to begin with can make them feel successful and show other students that they are a contributing member of the class.

Some children may need to be prompted through the job either by an adult or other students until they become familiar with what they need to do.

teacher's script

Say, "It's fun to get to do class jobs, especially when they get you out of class for a few minutes. But it's also important to take the job seriously and when you are doing a job outside the classroom remember that you represent everyone in your class. When you do a good job, teachers and students are proud of you."

class jobs
student page

date _____

time _____

setting _____

teacher _____

period _____

student name _____

_____

self-talk story

I like to do the job given to me by my teacher. Some jobs I like to do better than others, but I will do all of the jobs as best as I know how. I have to remember to follow the school rules when I walk to the office or do another job outside of the classroom. If I am responsible the teacher will be pleased. If I forget what I am supposed to do the teacher may assign someone to help me or tell me herself so that I can finish my job.

self-monitoring checklist

M	T	W	R	F	
☐	☐	☐	☐	☐	1. I learn each job by watching others do it.
☐	☐	☐	☐	☐	2. I do jobs without complaint.
☐	☐	☐	☐	☐	3. I pay attention until done.
☐	☐	☐	☐	☐	4. I obey school rules when I am out of class.
☐	☐	☐	☐	☐	5. If I forget how to do the job I ask teacher.

my story

M	T	W	R	F
☐	☐	☐	☐	☐
☐	☐	☐	☐	☐
☐	☐	☐	☐	☐
☐	☐	☐	☐	☐
☐	☐	☐	☐	☐

_____

_____

_____

_____

_____

four

breaks and special events

skills

lunch break

teacher guidelines

narrative

Getting lunch in the cafeteria line is a pleasant and uneventful routine for most students. However, the cafeteria can prove a difficult place for children who are overwhelmed by noise and movement and prone to stimulus overload.

In addition, students who have difficulty controlling their impulses may find waiting in line for even a short period trying. Cutting in, excess voice volume and other acting out behaviors are not uncommon during lunch period. Also, children should be encouraged to thank the food servers.

objective

When in the lunchroom the student will go through the line according to cafeteria rules.

benchmarks

1. S will stand in line.

2. S will talk to friends in a normal voice and engage in appropriate school conversation.

3. S will wait patiently in line.

4. S will be polite to the food servers.

5. S will walk directly to assigned area to eat.

problem checklist

Once the routine for how to interact in the lunch line has been learned most students perform this task well. Most of the problems arise while waiting for a turn in line and some students should practice interacting with food servers and learning to observe other rules such as how much food to take.

teacher's script

Say, "Lunch is a time to relax and enjoy yourself, but you still have to obey school rules. Wait your turn in line without cutting or pushing and be polite to cafeteria workers."

lunch break

student page

having lunch

date _____

time _____

setting _____

teacher _____

period _____

student name _____

_____

self-talk story

While in the cafeteria I must remember to stay in my place and to talk in a normal classroom voice. I can talk about things that are appropriate in school. When the line is long it is hard to wait but I have to remember not to yell at the people in front of me or push then to get the line to move faster. I take the food I need and thank the people serving the food. When my tray is full I walk directly to the area assigned to my class.

self-monitoring checklist

M	T	W	R	F	
☐	☐	☐	☐	☐	1. I stay in place in line.
☐	☐	☐	☐	☐	2. I talk in a normal voice.
☐	☐	☐	☐	☐	3. I wait patiently for my turn.
☐	☐	☐	☐	☐	4. I thank food server.
☐	☐	☐	☐	☐	5. I go to the area were my class sits.

my story

M	T	W	R	F
☐	☐	☐	☐	☐
☐	☐	☐	☐	☐
☐	☐	☐	☐	☐
☐	☐	☐	☐	☐
☐	☐	☐	☐	☐

_____

_____

_____

_____

eating skills

teacher guidelines

narrative

Table manners have been in decline for years. With family sit-down dinners held less and less often, and more visits to fast food places common, how to conduct oneself in a public eating place is a social skill that many students are not being taught. Children who talk with their mouths full of food, who have sauce smeared on their faces, or who grab food off of other children's trays do not endear themselves to their friends.

Students who do not clean up their eating area irritate the food staff and leave a poor impression of themselves.

Table manners include proper and appropriate communication skills.

objective

When in the cafeteria the student will use the proper utensils, chew with his mouth closed, ask before sharing food with a friend, use the napkin correctly, use appropriate communication skills, and clean up the eating area before leaving the lunchroom.

benchmarks

1. S will use the proper utensils.

2. S will eat with his/her mouth closed.

3. S will ask to share food with a friend.

4. S will use napkin to wipe face and hands.

5. S will clean up eating area including spills.

problem checklist

There are a few children who have not been taught even the basic eating skills. These children may benefit from a "lunch bunch" group, which is taught by an adult.

Students who do not understand the social rules for eating may have to have their checklist changed into a social story with a photo of them doing the skills and having that read before going to the cafeteria, (e.g., children with autism).

teacher's script

Say, "Eating with your friends is fun when you use proper table manners, like using the right silverware, eating with your mouth closed, wiping your face with a napkin and cleaning up your area before you leave."

eating skills

student page

eating lunch

date _____

time _____

setting _____

teacher _____

period _____

student name _____

_____

self-talk story

My friends like to have lunch with me when I follow the rules for eating. I must use my knife, fork and spoon the right way. I have to remember not to talk when I have food in my mouth. If one of my friends has food to share, I have to remember to ask before taking anything off of another person's tray. When I am finished I use my napkin to wipe my face and hands. Before leaving the lunchroom I look to clean up any mess that I have made while eating.

self-monitoring checklist

M	T	W	R	F
☐	☐	☐	☐	☐
☐	☐	☐	☐	☐
☐	☐	☐	☐	☐
☐	☐	☐	☐	☐
☐	☐	☐	☐	☐

1. I use utensils correctly.
2. I eat with mouth closed.
3. I ask before taking food from others.
4. I use a napkin if needed.
5. I clean my place when done.

my story

M	T	W	R	F
☐	☐	☐	☐	☐
☐	☐	☐	☐	☐
☐	☐	☐	☐	☐
☐	☐	☐	☐	☐
☐	☐	☐	☐	☐

_____

_____

_____

_____

_____

coming in from recess

teacher guidelines

narrative

Transitions are hard for some children. For those who enjoy playing with their friends, coming quietly into the classroom can be especially difficult. They struggle with calming down and can disrupt others by being too loud or active.

Children who may have had a conflict on the playground can enter the building still arguing or fuming to themselves and make it difficult for those around them. These children need to learn how to calm down before they come inside. Then, it is easier for them to talk about and deal with the conflict.

objective

When the signal that recess is over is heard the student will stop playing and follow the procedure for transitioning from playground to classroom.

benchmarks

1. S will stop playing when the signal that recess is over is sounded.

2. S will line up in the designated area (with any borrowed playground equipment).

3. S will lower voice before entering the building.

4. S will put all personal items in assigned area in the hallway.

5. S will quietly enter the classroom, sit down and wait for the teacher's directions.

problem checklist

Children who have conflicts on the playground may need to have an extra step so that they can find a place to calm down before they enter the classroom. It is hard for students to make a successful transition when they are angry. These children may need to have adult guidance and extra verbal praise for following a set procedure that will allow them to make transitions successfully.

teacher's script

Say, "Recess is a lot of fun because you get a chance to play with your friends and let off some of your energy. But when it's over, you have to calm down, quiet down and slow down before you enter your class again."

coming in from recess

date _____

time _____

setting _____

teacher _____

period _____

student name _____

_____

self-talk story

I get excited playing with my friends on the playground and it is hard to stop playing when I hear the bell ring. I return the playground equipment I brought out with me and line up with my class. I remember to lower my voice before I come inside. I take off my coat and hang it up on my hook in the hallway. I talk quietly to my friend as I enter the classroom and sit down at my desk. I wait for my teacher to give us the next direction.

self-monitoring checklist

M	T	W	R	F	
☐	☐	☐	☐	☐	1. I come when I hear bell or other signal.
☐	☐	☐	☐	☐	2. I return playground equipment I used.
☐	☐	☐	☐	☐	3. I lower my voice inside school.
☐	☐	☐	☐	☐	4. I put personal items in my cubby.
☐	☐	☐	☐	☐	5. I enter class and wait for directions.

my story

M	T	W	R	F
☐	☐	☐	☐	☐
☐	☐	☐	☐	☐
☐	☐	☐	☐	☐
☐	☐	☐	☐	☐
☐	☐	☐	☐	☐

_____

_____

_____

_____

_____

knowing recess rules

teacher guidelines

narrative

Recess can be a time of fun and excitement or one where conflict and disagreements arise. It can even be a time of dread for those students who do not have good gross motor or communicative skills, or who haven't had the opportunity to learn group sports and feel inferior because they do not possess good game-playing skills.

Children with sensory problems, such as those with autism and hyperactivity disorders, can be overloaded by the sound and activity on a playground.

For students who have trouble making friends, recess can be a lonely time that accentuates negative feelings they already have about themselves.

In order to save face, some students with the above challenges react by becoming overly aggressive, thus isolating themselves even further. In addition, students for whom recess is a miserable experience may bring that back to class with them. Resolving playground problems can become a daily occurrence for the classroom teacher.

objective

During recess the student will play in a safe and appropriate way according to game or activity rules and general school recess rules.

benchmarks

1. S plays in ways that are safe for others.
2. S follows game and equipment rules.
3. S negotiates conflicts appropriately.
4. S listens to playground supervisor.
5. S walks to and from playground in an orderly fashion.

problem checklist

Some children attempt to participate in group games but are not successful because of either poor gross motor skills or because they haven't had the opportunity to play the game. It can be helpful to have an older student (tutor) come during recess to give them a chance to learn game skills.

Children with sensory issues benefit from a group of peers willing to play with them and to have a place to go for recess on days when their sensory system is on overload.

Children whose behavior interferes with peer interactions may have to develop social skills which emphasize playing in a safe way, learning to take turns, adhering to game rules, compromising and listening to playground supervisors. For these students each skill may have to be addressed separately before a child can be successful on the playground.

teacher's script

Say, "Recess is a break in your day that can be fun and exciting, but it's still part of the school day and you need to obey the rules of recess. Play in a way that is safe for you and others. Play by the rules of the game you are playing. Listen to the playground teachers and aides and when it's over return to the school directly. If you do these things, you will have fun at recess."

knowing recess rules

student page

date _____

time _____

setting _____

teacher _____

period _____

student name _____

_____

self-talk story

It is time for recess and I walk outside with my friend. Whatever we do together, we take turns and don't fight about it. I remember to follow the rules for playing safe. I compromise so I don't argue with my friend. I listen to and follow directions from the playground supervisors. When the bell rings I stop playing and walk back to class.

self-monitoring checklist

M	T	W	R	F
☐	☐	☐	☐	☐
☐	☐	☐	☐	☐
☐	☐	☐	☐	☐
☐	☐	☐	☐	☐
☐	☐	☐	☐	☐

1. I play safely so I don't hurt myself or others.
2. I take turns and obey game rules.
3. I compromise with others.
4. I listen to recess supervisor.
5. I leave when the bell rings.

my story

M	T	W	R	F
☐	☐	☐	☐	☐
☐	☐	☐	☐	☐
☐	☐	☐	☐	☐
☐	☐	☐	☐	☐
☐	☐	☐	☐	☐

_____

_____

_____

_____

_____

twenty-seven

crisis drills

teacher guidelines

narrative

Emergency evacuations such as fire, tornado, and crisis drills do not occur on a daily basis and children who have body space problems, or who cannot follow directions well can struggle with them. Since drills are not a typical part of the school day, the sudden announcement that one is taking place can upset students who cannot manage a sudden change in their daily routine. Loud noises or close proximity of other students is often uncomfortable for students who have sensory problems. In order for them to comply with safety rules these drills need to be foreshadowed (so students understand the procedure before they are involved in it). Foreshadowing can't be done without forewarning from the administration that an emergency evacuation will be occurring. Ask your administration to give you advance notice.

For students who don't have sensory issues, drills can still pose the usual discipline problems caused by unusual situations. Every student must understand that drills are rehearsals for potentially serious events and are to be treated as such.

objective

During a crisis drill the student will listen to directions, move calmly to the designated area and remain quiet until appropriate staff members say it's over.

benchmarks

1. S will quietly listen to the PA announcement for the drill.

2. S will listen to teacher directions.

3. S will go to the designated area (which will depend on the nature of the drill).

4. S will remain quiet throughout the drill.

5. S will return to his seat when the PA announcement states the drill is over.

problem checklist

For children who have problems sitting in a group, a space on the outside of the group can be assigned. Children with tactile defensiveness may need to have some kind of soft ball or toy to squeeze in order for them to tolerate the close proximity of other students, whether waiting in line for the outdoor drills or huddled on the floor for the crisis drill.

teacher's script

Say, "We don't have fire, tornado or crisis drills everyday, so they are a little different from other school events. But they are important because we are learning how to act if something serious happens in school. For this reason, you must take them seriously and do what the staff asks you and remain quiet while the drills are happening."

crisis drills
student page

crisis
drills

date _____

time _____

setting _____

teacher _____

period _____

student name _____

_____

self-talk story

During crisis drills I need to pay attention to my teacher and not talk to my friends. After the PA announcement I must listen to my teacher. I walk to the safe area and sit down on the floor. It is hard but I must remember not to talk or to push other students. I must be quiet so that I can hear what my teacher might need to tell me. When the all clear signal is given over the PA I must listen to my teacher. When she tells me it's okay, then I can go back to my seat.

self-monitoring checklist

M	T	W	R	F
☐	☐	☐	☐	☐
☐	☐	☐	☐	☐
☐	☐	☐	☐	☐
☐	☐	☐	☐	☐
☐	☐	☐	☐	☐

1. I listen to announcement.
2. I obey teacher.
3. I am calm and quiet.
4. I don't push others.
5. I return when the teacher says.

my story

M	T	W	R	F
☐	☐	☐	☐	☐
☐	☐	☐	☐	☐
☐	☐	☐	☐	☐
☐	☐	☐	☐	☐
☐	☐	☐	☐	☐

_____

_____

_____

_____

_____

going to the nurse

teacher guidelines

narrative

These days, there seems to be many children who have to go to the nurse's office for some kind of daily medication. The teacher and child should be aware of the time the medication is supposed to be given. Discretion and confidentiality are the keywords: Teachers should never announce in front of the entire class that a child needs to get his medication. Instead, the teacher can post the time somewhere in the classroom, in a subtle fashion, to cue the child of his medication time.

Some days the nurse's office can be very busy and for children who have poor social skills waiting their turn can be difficult.

For younger children or those with verbal or other communicative disabilities, learning how to ask for assistance is very helpful and can lead to more independence.

objective

The student will go to and return from the nurse's office at the scheduled time.

benchmarks

1. S will be aware of the posted time to go to the nurse's office.

2. S will walk directly to the office.

3. S will look to see if the nurse is busy and wait quietly for his/her turn.

4. S will greet the nurse and state needs.

5. S will thank the nurse and walk back to the classroom.

problem checklist

If the time that the student needs to see the nurse follows a scheduled daily routine, it's helpful to cue the child to get his medication after a particular activity that precedes it. For example, if his medication time is between language arts and math each day, cue him to go at that time.

For emergencies, like an injury on the playground, it is helpful for the student to learn how to interrupt politely in order for the nurse to attend to his injury.

teacher's script

Say, "Most of you end up in the Nurse's office sometime during the school year and some have to go often to get your medications. If you go there for an emergency, like a cut you got on the playground, or when you're sick and you need to go home, you may interrupt the nurse if you do it politely. If you go there for medications, know your schedule, go there directly and be polite to the nurse. When you're done, return immediately to your classroom."

going to the nurse

student page

date _____

time _____

setting _____

teacher _____

period _____

student name _____

_____

self-talk story

I must remember what time to go to the Nurse's office for my medications. When I go there, I follow school rules for walking in the hallway. I look to see if the person in the office is busy and I wait my turn. When it is my turn, I say "Hello (and the person's name). I need to get my medication." I thank the person in the office and walk back to my classroom.

self-monitoring checklist

M	T	W	R	F	
☐	☐	☐	☐	☐	1. I check my schedule so I'm not late.
☐	☐	☐	☐	☐	2. I walk straight to nurse's office.
☐	☐	☐	☐	☐	3. I wait turn my if the nurse is busy.
☐	☐	☐	☐	☐	4. I greet her and say what I need.
☐	☐	☐	☐	☐	5. I thank her and return to class.

my story

M	T	W	R	F	
☐	☐	☐	☐	☐	_____
☐	☐	☐	☐	☐	_____
☐	☐	☐	☐	☐	_____
☐	☐	☐	☐	☐	_____
☐	☐	☐	☐	☐	_____

field trips

teacher guidelines

narrative

Fields trips are often exciting and truly can be educational because students appreciate the extra effort involved and usually pay attention. Proper behavior by the class helps make the trip enjoyable.

However, to encourage this outcome, it helps to provide some foreshadowing for your students. Before you leave, explain the purpose of the field trip and the rules for behavior to the students. For example, what is expected of the audience at a classical music concert is different from that at a comedy. There are different rules for behavior in a museum than at a water park. Children need to be properly prepared for what is expected of them and when they are, their behavior usually reflects it.

objective

When on a field trip the student will understand the purpose of the trip and follow class rules for behavior.

benchmarks

1. S states the purpose of the trip.

2. S brings required materials (e.g., bagged lunch or warm clothing).

3. When in a line, S stays in own place and talks in a quiet voice.

4. S looks at and follows the directions of the teacher or tour guide.

5. S cleans up areas used by the class and thanks the tour guide, chaperones, bus driver, etc.

problem checklist

It is important that children can verbalize the rules for behavior before they go on the field trip and again before they disembark from the bus. There are specific rules for walking in a wildlife preserve, such as staying on the trails and speaking quietly so as not to scare away the wildlife. In museums children need to be careful not to touch displays unless given permission by the tour guide. Rules in a water park would emphasize playing safely.

For some children, specific objectives and benchmarks may need to be written to fit the trip planned by the class.

It's also important for them to thank tour guides, parent volunteers, and the bus driver — any adults who were involved in their experience. Children who follow the rules of etiquette leave a good impression of their school.

teacher's script

Say, "Field trips are a chance to get out of school and do something fun while you're learning about it. If you obey the rules of field trips and are polite to the adults that help you enjoy it, you will have a really good time."

field trips
student page

taking field trips

date _____

time _____

setting _____

teacher _____

period _____

student name _____

_____

self-talk story

Today I am going with my class on a field trip. I checked to be sure that I have my lunch and the right clothes, like my jacket, if I need it. I stand in line by my friends but I remember not to talk too loud. I look at and follow directions once we get there. I thank adults who helped us enjoy our field trip and the driver as I get off the bus.

self-monitoring checklist

M T W R F

□ □ □ □ □   1. I know where we're going and why.
□ □ □ □ □   2. I take my lunch and dress right for weather.
□ □ □ □ □   3. I use a normal voice.
□ □ □ □ □   4. I follow directions.
□ □ □ □ □   5. I thank guides and drivers.

my story

M T W R F

□ □ □ □ □   _____
□ □ □ □ □   _____
□ □ □ □ □   _____
□ □ □ □ □   _____
□ □ □ □ □   _____

going to the bathroom

teacher guidelines

narrative

Elementary school students are constantly making trips to the bathroom, but monitoring the bathroom is not easy for a teacher who has to remain in the classroom. Since bathrooms are physically separate areas where adults often are not present, they are places where mischief can easily occur and frequently does.

Teaching children to walk the hallways and use facilities properly can prevent complaints about behavior. Using timed passes or allowing only one child at a time out of the classroom can prevent social gatherings there. Children should also know the acceptable times they are allowed to leave the classroom. Unless it is an emergency, most children can wait until a teacher presentation is over before leaving the classroom.

objective

Will follow classroom rules for asking and going to and from the bathroom within a specified time limit.

benchmarks

1. S will ask for permission to leave the classroom.

2. S will walk directly to the bathroom.

3. S will speak in a normal voice when in the bathroom.

4. S will flush the toilet, wash hands and put paper in the trash bin.

5. S walks back to the classroom within the allotted time period.

problem checklist

Certain students can use a bathroom trip as an excuse to avoid completing work. Teachers should limited the number of times each student goes per day and find ways to assist that child during academic times so that they develop more competencies and spend less time avoiding the work.

Some children who are sensitive about noises can find bathrooms overwhelming because the harsh acoustic environment (tiles, metal stalls, etc.) can amplify normal levels of sound. These children may have to have times scheduled in their school day for bathroom breaks when the facility is not crowded to ease the noise level for them.

Some children with certain disabilities may have to have a visual cue on their pass to help them remember important steps (e.g., a picture of a pair of hands under a water faucet).

teacher's script

Say, "You will need to use the restroom often during the school week. When you do you need to let your teacher know, go straight there, use a normal voice and clean up after yourself. Then you must come straight back to class. If you do these things, you won't disturb others and everyone will be proud of you."

going to the bathroom

student page

going to the bathroom

date _____

time _____

setting _____

teacher _____

period _____

student name _____

_____

self-talk story

I ask the teacher in a normal voice if I can go to the bathroom. I get the pass and walk there myself. I see my friend and I remember to say hello in a normal voice. Before I leave the bathroom I flush the toilet, wash my hands, and put the paper towel in the wastebasket. I walk quietly back to my classroom on time.

self-monitoring checklist

M	T	W	R	F	
☐	☐	☐	☐	☐	1. I ask politely to go.
☐	☐	☐	☐	☐	2. I walk straight there.
☐	☐	☐	☐	☐	3. I use a normal voice.
☐	☐	☐	☐	☐	4. I flush, wash and put the towel in trash.
☐	☐	☐	☐	☐	5. I go directly back to class.

my story

M	T	W	R	F	
☐	☐	☐	☐	☐	_____
☐	☐	☐	☐	☐	_____
☐	☐	☐	☐	☐	_____
☐	☐	☐	☐	☐	_____
☐	☐	☐	☐	☐	_____

five
anyplace

skills

greeting teachers

teacher guidelines

narrative

Many children walk down the hallway or onto the playground and do not acknowledge adult staff whom they know. It is often considered "uncool" to greet adults with whom they are familiar, such as former teachers. This is especially common among older elementary students. Teachers often complain about this behavior, but schools seldom addresses it. Yet there are compelling reasons to encourage it. Positive social skills in areas like this have long-term beneficial results for students by allowing them to bond and form productive relationships with staff members. Just as academic skills have to be taught early, so do the rules of social etiquette.

objective

The student will greet an adult staff person they know in the school building and on the school grounds.

benchmarks

1. S will greet the classroom teacher.

2. S will greet support staff, food service workers and custodians whom they encounter on a daily basis.

3. S will learn the distinction between greeting familiar adults and those they do not know as well.

4. S will use the formal Mr., Mrs., or Ms. with the adult's last name, unless requested by the adult to do otherwise.

5. Or, S will address the adult according to how they have been instructed by that adult.

problem checklist

Children who are skilled in rules of social etiquette help add a warmer and more friendly environment to the school community. Children from all different backgrounds need to be taught the difference between public behavior and private behavior. In other words, how you acknowledge school staff (public behavior) is different from greeting your friends or even family members (private behavior). Children who do not possess these skills may need to be taught in smaller steps such as smiling and saying "Hi."

Some parent volunteers or older students who come into the school to do tutoring may feel comfortable having the children use their first name. Children need to learn the differences between knowing an adult well outside of school and the people who work in the school.

teacher's script

Say, "When you see teachers and other adults in the school who you know, greet them with respect. Say 'hi' and use Mr., Mrs., Ms. and their last name. This is the right thing to do and it makes adults happy with you and it makes school a more pleasant place to be for everyone."

greeting teachers

student page

date _____

time _____

setting _____

teacher _____

period _____

student name _____

_____

greeting teachers and other staff

self-talk story

When I see my teacher I do not have to wait for her to say "hello" to me. I can smile and say "Hi (and her name) or "Good morning." I can stop to talk to my teacher if she is not busy. When I go to the office I can say hello to the secretary. Unless an adult has given me permission to use her first name, I need to always greet them by saying Mr. or Mrs. followed by their last name. Adults like it when I am polite to them.

self-monitoring checklist

M T W R F

1. I smile and greet my teacher.
2. I greet other adults I know.
3. I use Mr. or Ms. and their last name.
4. I just say "hi" to adults I don't know.
5. I use first names only if adults tell me it's okay.

my story

M T W R F

_____

_____

_____

_____

_____

asking for help
teacher guidelines

narrative

Teaching children how to ask for help appropriately is an essential skill. Some students do not turn in completed work because they do not understand how to do the assignment. They can look like children who refuse to do work rather than as those who do not know how to do it.

While some children may be very shy about asking for help, they must master this skill for those times when they have a question.

Other students tend to just blurt out a question and can disturb their classmates during quiet work times.

Students with disabilities often need to be taught how to ask appropriately for help.

Some may simply act out in frustration because they don't know how to go about asking for assistance.

objective

Every time the student needs help from the teacher he/she will raise a hand.

benchmarks

1. S will look at the teacher and quietly raise a hand.

2. S will remain quiet while her hand is in the air.

3. S will remain calm until the teacher calls on her.

4. S will speak in a normal voice.

5. S will thank the teacher for helping.

problem checklist

Some students become so anxious that they wave their hand about or will start to talk out before the teacher has time to call on them. One way of reducing blurting out is to praise children who are following the rules. For example, as soon as the student who tends to blurt attempts to raise his hand appropriately, praise him.

Some students with disabilities may need to have the steps broken down into smaller increments before they understand what is expected of them.

A smaller group of children with disabilities, such as autism — which often impedes initiating social interaction — may not be able to look at or address the teacher directly at all. These children will need extra guidance to master this skill, or a classroom modification or adaptation to help them achieve it.

teacher's script

Say, "Everyone needs help once in a while, and it's important to know how to ask for it. First, look at the teacher and raise your hand, then wait patiently for her to call on you. When she does, ask for help in a normal voice, and when she's done, thank her. That way you'll get the help you need and the teacher will be happy to give it to you."

asking for help

student page

date _____

time _____

setting _____

teacher _____

period _____

student name _____

_____

self-talk story

If I talk out loud without permission it is hard for my teacher to hear another student asking a question. I need to remember that if I have a question, I look at my teacher and raise my hand. I need to stay calm and wait for her to call on me. If my teacher calls on me I talk in a normal classroom voice. I can thank my teacher for helping me. It makes her happy when I follow the rules.

self-monitoring checklist

M	T	W	R	F
☐	☐	☐	☐	☐
☐	☐	☐	☐	☐
☐	☐	☐	☐	☐
☐	☐	☐	☐	☐
☐	☐	☐	☐	☐

1. I look at the teacher and raise hand.
2. I stay quiet until called.
3. I wait if the teacher is busy.
4. I use a normal voice.
5. I thank the teacher for helping me.

my story

M	T	W	R	F
☐	☐	☐	☐	☐
☐	☐	☐	☐	☐
☐	☐	☐	☐	☐
☐	☐	☐	☐	☐
☐	☐	☐	☐	☐

_____

_____

_____

_____

_____

_____

respecting body space
teacher guidelines

narrative

Young children like to hug people and impulsively touch objects which belong to others. In a group situation, some children brush up against other students because they don't always understand the unwritten rules for giving others their body space.

Other students may shrink from touching people and need to know when it is appropriate to allow someone to touch them.

Toys and other objects brought to school can cause conflicts because students like to play with them. When children grab items that do not belong to them, problems occur.

Some need to learn that opening others' book bags or desks without getting permission is not proper behavior. Teaching children when it is proper to keep hands to themselves, and when it is okay to touch people or objects, helps create a classroom of mutual respect.

objective

When in the school building the student will keep hands to self unless given permission to touch objects or others.

benchmarks

1. S will respect the body space of others in a group situation.

2. S will know the difference between touching in a friendly manner and touching impulsively or to annoy another.

3. S will apologize for inadvertently touching someone.

4. S will get permission to use someone else's belongings.

5. S will respect other people's personal property when using it.

problem checklist

Children with autism tend to lean into the body space of others. They seem to need that contact to help guide them in a group situation. Like all children, they need to learn the rules for when it is okay to touch people in a friendly manner. Using a carpet piece or a taped area on the floor (or around the desk) of a child with autism can provide a visual cue. It also helps to prepare the child with a social script.

Teach impulsive children how to ask for permission to play with or borrow the property of others. And don't forget to teach them how to accept a refusal from other children. Conversely, all children should understand that sometimes it is okay for them to refuse others to touch or borrow their possessions.

Some students also need to be taught school rules for leaving hall or IMC displays alone.

teacher's script

Say, "Nothing starts a fight faster than touching other people or their things without asking them. When you are near other kids, like standing in line, be careful to give them enough room. Don't touch people on purpose unless you know it is okay with them. If you do it by accident, apologize. Never touch other kids things without getting their permission first. If you follow these rules, you will avoid getting in fights and arguments."

respecting body space

student page

keep hands to self

date _____

time _____

setting _____

teacher _____

period _____

student name _____

_____

self-talk story

When I am standing near other kids, like waiting in line, it is hard to stand straight and not lean on my friend or the wall. I can talk to my friends but I have to remember that it can make them angry if I keep hanging on them. I also need to remember not to touch the posters on the wall made by the art class. I must keep my feet off of the wall and hands by my side while standing in line.

self-monitoring checklist

M	T	W	R	F	
☐	☐	☐	☐	☐	1. I respect body space around others.
☐	☐	☐	☐	☐	2. I know when it's okay to touch others.
☐	☐	☐	☐	☐	3. If I bump someone, I apologize.
☐	☐	☐	☐	☐	4. When borrowing from friends I ask if it's okay.
☐	☐	☐	☐	☐	5. I respect others' things.

my story

M	T	W	R	F
☐	☐	☐	☐	☐
☐	☐	☐	☐	☐
☐	☐	☐	☐	☐
☐	☐	☐	☐	☐
☐	☐	☐	☐	☐

_____

_____

_____

_____

_____

responding to teasing
teacher guidelines

narrative

Teasing seems to be on the increase in schools. Teaching children how to respond to teasing helps reduce incidents and empower students. Children feel good about themselves when they can come up with a plan they have thought out, and it works. When the child who is the object of teasing can respond with firmness often the teaser will stop.

Children with disabilities are frequently the subject of taunts regarding their handicaps. Dealing with them, especially in the era of inclusion, often requires attending to the specific nature of the teasing. If it has become a pronounced problem, you may need to address it with the entire class, with or without the students with disabilities present.

objective

When constantly teased by another the student will develop, practice and implement a plan to stop the teasing.

benchmarks

1. S will stop and think whether or not to respond to the situation.

2. S will develop a plan.

3. S will practice the plan.

4. S will make eye contact and implement the plan.

5. S will talk in a firm vice when addressing his grievance.

problem checklist

Children need to learn to distinguish between occasional and constant teasing.

Children need to learn to distinguish between a humorous friendly comment and teasing that is intended to be hurtful.

Children need to learn that several different plans may need to be tried out before they are successful in stopping the teasing from occurring. A plan that works for one kind of teasing may not work for all kinds. Learning how to use humor to derail teasing is helpful.

Sometimes students with disabilities, or significantly different cultural backgrounds, can be subjects for teasing. If this is the situation, the school staff may need to intervene and educate the teasers as to why that child is different, and to communicate that the teasing will stop or consequences given. There is a distinction between teasing and harassment. No one should have to deal with harassment on a daily basis.

Sometimes students with disabilities are so hypersensitive they may imagine that the normal teasing of children is directed against their handicaps even when it isn't. When this is the case, they need to be reminded that (while an unattractive practice) teasing is a normal behavior of children and need not always be about their disability.

teacher's script

Say, "Nobody likes to be teased. It makes you mad and hurts your feelings. But it happens a lot in school so you need to have a plan to deal with it. Your teacher or some other adult can help you with your plan. When your plan works, you will feel safer and a lot happier."

responding to teasing

student page

coming up with a plan

date _____

time _____

setting _____

teacher _____

period _____

student name _____

_____

self-talk story

When I am at school some kids tease me. Teasing makes me upset because it happens a lot. But now I have a plan to stop it. I practiced my plan, too. Next time when someone teases me I will remain calm and follow my plan. When I talk to the person I will look at their face and keep my voice normal.

self-monitoring checklist

M	T	W	R	F
☐	☐	☐	☐	☐
☐	☐	☐	☐	☐
☐	☐	☐	☐	☐
☐	☐	☐	☐	☐
☐	☐	☐	☐	☐

1. I know when I need to do something about it.
2. I make a plan to deal with it.
3. If needed, I ask adults for help.
4. I practice and follow my plan.
5. I talk in a normal but firm voice.

my story

M	T	W	R	F
☐	☐	☐	☐	☐
☐	☐	☐	☐	☐
☐	☐	☐	☐	☐
☐	☐	☐	☐	☐
☐	☐	☐	☐	☐

_____

_____

_____

_____

_____

being responsible
teacher guidelines

narrative

Every teacher has had a student who can never find something when it is needed. While children who are "organizationally challenged" are often endearing types, instruction is held up while they look in vain for school materials.

In addition, lost personal items can bring on distress because the student becomes frustrated about where the item was put. Messy desks, lockers, or cubbies make it even more difficult for children with organizational problems to find what they need.

In addition, there are often social consequences for children who hold up class activities or have lost valuable personal items.

objective

The student will keep all personal items and school materials in a designated area which is organized on a daily basis.

benchmarks

1. S decides what items to bring to school each day and puts them in a backpack.

2. S puts all school materials in the desk.

3. S keeps desk organized so school related materials can be found quickly.

4. S takes responsibility for all personal items and school related materials.

5. S cleans up and makes sure nothing is left behind before leaving to do another task.

problem checklist

There are some children who in spite of all attempts to organize still have messy desks or lockers. These children may need constant interventions until they're able to learn the rudiments of being organized.

A weekly cleaning of desks and cubbies with assistance from another student, parent volunteer, or other available adult is a must.

Also verbally rewarding the student's attempts to be organized is helpful in giving the student an incentive for being responsible for his materials.

teacher's script

Say, "Everyday you need to bring some of your own things to school, like pencils and notebooks and your jacket. It's important to keep track of them yourself. Then when you need them, you can find them."

being responsible

student page

date _____

time _____

setting _____

teacher _____

period _____

student name _____

_____

keep track of your stuff

self-talk story

I put all of my homework in my backpack. I decide to leave my computer game at home because it is expensive and I don't want to lose it. I put my take home folder and homework in my desk. After each subject I put the worksheet and packets in the correct folders so that I can find them later and do not hold up the class looking for what I need. Before I leave school, I check around my seat to be sure that nothing is on the floor and all of my belongings have been put into my desk.

self-monitoring checklist

M	T	W	R	F
☐	☐	☐	☐	☐
☐	☐	☐	☐	☐
☐	☐	☐	☐	☐
☐	☐	☐	☐	☐
☐	☐	☐	☐	☐

1. I remember to take what I need to school.
2. I put my things where they belong.
3. I take responsibility for my things.
4. I don't blame others if they get lost.
5. I keep my area clean.

my story

M	T	W	R	F
☐	☐	☐	☐	☐
☐	☐	☐	☐	☐
☐	☐	☐	☐	☐
☐	☐	☐	☐	☐
☐	☐	☐	☐	☐

_____

_____

_____

_____

_____

thirty-six

making an apology
teacher guidelines

narrative

It is often difficult for adults to apologize for their behavior, so it's not hard to understand why children also struggle with making an apology. But students in a classroom need to understand that apologizing for hurting someone else's feelings leads to having more friends and makes the classroom atmosphere more relaxed. Children learn better when not angry or feeling hurt.

objective

The student will apologize to another person every time he makes a hurtful statement or commits a harmful act.

benchmarks

1. S asks to talk to the person.

2. S makes eye contact.

3. S says: "I am sorry for saying, or doing" (whatever). I hope that you can accept my apology."

4. S waits for the other person to respond.

5. S smiles and says thank you and shakes hands if appropriate.

problem checklist

Some children may at first find it difficult to talk to the person whose feelings have been hurt. In order to develop this skill these students may need to use a keyboarding device to type a letter or write an e-mail. It's important to gradually move children toward making a face-to-face contact after they have learned how to make a written apology.

Not only do children need to learn how to respond to an apology that has been accepted, they also need to learn how to handle a rebuff of their attempt to apologize. A teacher needs to assist children to learn ways to manage their own hurt feeling when an apology is refused.

teacher's script

Say, "It's hard to apologize to someone when you said or did something that made them feel bad. But think about how you feel when somebody does that to you. It's important to learn to apologize and usually when you do, it makes other people really happy with you."

making an apology
student page

making an apology

date _____

time _____

setting _____

teacher _____

period _____

student name _____

_____

self-talk story

I feel sad that I hurt my friend's feelings. I still want him/her to be my friend and I need to say that I am sorry for hurting his/her feelings.

self-monitoring checklist

M	T	W	R	F	
☐	☐	☐	☐	☐	1. I ask to talk to the person.
☐	☐	☐	☐	☐	2. I look the person in the eye.
☐	☐	☐	☐	☐	3. I say I am sorry.
☐	☐	☐	☐	☐	4. I wait for the response.
☐	☐	☐	☐	☐	5. I thank the person for listening.

my story

M	T	W	R	F
☐	☐	☐	☐	☐
☐	☐	☐	☐	☐
☐	☐	☐	☐	☐
☐	☐	☐	☐	☐
☐	☐	☐	☐	☐

_____

_____

_____

_____

_____

voice volume
teacher guidelines

narrative

When in a group, children often can't resist talking to each other. But, in their excitement they can become too noisy. For example, group project work has a tendency to be louder than normal classroom noise.

Some children entering the building from the playground chronically forget to lower their voices and can disturb other classrooms unintentionally. As a result they can find themselves disciplined for being too loud.

Other students have naturally loud voices or ones that are so soft they are hard to hear in a classroom setting. These children seem to have their volume stuck at one level. It is helpful to teach these students how and when it is appropriate to change their voice volume.

objective

When in different school environments the student will use an appropriate voice volume.

benchmarks

1. S will monitor own voice volume.

2. S will speak in an acceptable volume when in the classroom.

3. S will lower voice when working in a group.

4. When the class is working S, will whisper when asking a classmate a question or to borrow materials.

5. S will know when it is okay to be louder than normal, such as on the playground, or when it is necessary to raise volume, such as when asking a question in class.

problem checklist

Children with a naturally loud voice may benefit from a nonverbal signal that cues them to speak softer.

Children with soft voices need to feel comfortable talking in a louder than normal voice in front of a class so all can hear. These students can also benefit from a nonverbal signal.

Children who have difficulty coming into a classroom after recess, or the lunchroom, may need to have a landmark cue (such as when they reach the fire hydrant or a planting of shrubs outside of the building) to help transition to a quieter environment.

teacher's script

Say, "Sometimes you need to speak louder for people to hear you, like on the playground or when you ask a question in class. Other times, it's important to speak softly so you don't disturb people around you. When you're careful about talking loud enough but not too loud, other people appreciate you trying so hard."

voice volume
student page

working
quietly
in the
classroom

date _____

time _____

setting _____

teacher _____

period _____

student name _____

_____

self-talk story

We are working quietly in the classroom. I ask to borrow a pair of scissors by whispering quietly to a classmate. I raise my hand when I have a question to ask. I talk to the teacher in a way that does not distract other children. At recess I talk louder on the playground. When I hear the signal that recess is over, I calm myself by the time I reach the school door. I walk into the school using a normal voice and do not disturb other students who may be working.

self-monitoring checklist

M	T	W	R	F	
☐	☐	☐	☐	☐	1. I know when to talk soft.
☐	☐	☐	☐	☐	2. I use a normal voice in class.
☐	☐	☐	☐	☐	3. I use a normal voice in groups.
☐	☐	☐	☐	☐	4. I whisper if I need something when someone is talking.
☐	☐	☐	☐	☐	5. I known when it's okay to be loud.

my story

M	T	W	R	F
☐	☐	☐	☐	☐
☐	☐	☐	☐	☐
☐	☐	☐	☐	☐
☐	☐	☐	☐	☐
☐	☐	☐	☐	☐

_____

_____

_____

_____

_____

accepting criticism

teacher guidelines

narrative

Teaching students to respond appropriately to criticism is one of the more difficult skills in this program. Adults struggle with accepting criticism, and for children it can be even more difficult. They often are extremely sensitive about what they see as negative feedback about themselves. As a result some may act out in an aggressive manner while others withdraw.

Nonetheless, children need to learn the difference between constructive criticisms and hurtful statements made in anger by others. Trying to help children manage hurt feelings is also part of learning to accept criticism. Teachers need to be aware of their own language when addressing student behavioral or academic problems.

objective

Will develop a plan for accepting constructive criticism from teachers and friends.

benchmarks

1. S will ask for assistance when necessary.

2. S will know the difference between constructive criticism and critical words.

3. S will recognize constructive words used by another.

4. S will be able to respond calmly to constructive criticism.

5. S will thank the person for helping.

problem checklist

Some children may need to learn the difference in the tone of voice and words used for constructive criticism. Teachers may have to role-play with these children so that they begin to learn the words and tone of voice and do not become defensive.

teacher's script

Say, "Criticism is when someone tells you something about yourself that can make you better. Sometimes it hurts your feelings. But, when a teacher or friend is trying to help you, it's important to listen carefully and not get angry or be hurt."

accepting criticism

student page

date _____

time _____

setting _____

teacher _____

period _____

student name _____

_____

learning to accept criticism

self-talk story

I am feeling frustrated and ask my friend to help me understand more about myself. Sometimes his words make me angry but I know that he is trying to help me. I try to listen to what he tells me. If I still don't understand I ask him to explain again. When he is finished I remember to thank him. Although I am feeling angry and upset I know that the words being said to me are helpful.

self-monitoring checklist

M	T	W	R	F
☐	☐	☐	☐	☐
☐	☐	☐	☐	☐
☐	☐	☐	☐	☐
☐	☐	☐	☐	☐
☐	☐	☐	☐	☐

1. I know when I need assistance.
2. I know when I'm wrong and can do better.
3. I recognize when the advice will be helpful.
4. I keep calm when criticized.
5. I listen and say 'thank you.'

my story

M	T	W	R	F
☐	☐	☐	☐	☐
☐	☐	☐	☐	☐
☐	☐	☐	☐	☐
☐	☐	☐	☐	☐
☐	☐	☐	☐	☐

_____

_____

_____

_____

_____

respecting teachers

teacher guidelines

narrative

A common complaint from teachers these days is the lack of respect students have for adults. Some students demand rather than ask for help and rarely use words of politeness such as please, thank you and you're welcome.

Others think nothing of walking between two teachers talking to each other in the hallway without excusing themselves, or ignore a teacher carrying an arm-load of materials into the building in order to get through the door first.

Listen to the conversation in the lounge and you will hear how often teachers complain about the "rudeness" they are seeing in today's children. Like any other skill taught in school, children need to learn how to interact respectfully with their teachers. Teachers do not need to accept lack of respect, since to do so is to encourage the development of bad habits by students.

It is worthy of consideration that students who possess and practice strong social skills in their relationships with adults benefit from an enhanced status among those staff members. In this era of slack social skills, the student who has them is empowered.

objective

The student will address her teacher with Mr., Mrs., Ms., and surname, will request help respectfully, wait her turn to talk to the teacher, follow directions and thank the teacher for helping.

benchmarks

1. S will address the teacher using a formal greeting.

2. S will request help rather than demand it.

3. S will wait her turn to talk to the teacher.

4. S will follow the teacher's directions.

5. S will thank the teacher for helping.

problem checklist

Some of your children will have such poorly developed social skills that the benchmarks may need to be broken down until each becomes an objective in itself.

It's important for you to give positive feedback to children who are trying to interact appropriately with you by acknowledging their socially proper behavior: e.g., "I like the way you ask me to help you. That's great the way you said, 'you're welcome to me." If you want respect, show the student the same respect.

teacher's script

Say, "When I see my teachers I will greet them in the right way as Mr., Mrs., or Ms., and use their last name. If I need help, I will ask politely and I will remember to thank them when they do help me. If I treat my teachers with respect they will like me and they will respect me, too."

respecting teachers

student page

date _____

time _____

setting _____

teacher _____

period _____

student name _____

_____

self-talk story

Every time I see my teachers I greet them with respect, even if I am with my friends. I say, "Hi, Mr., or Mrs., or Ms.," and use their last name. Sometimes I need help from my teachers. But teachers are busy and I must wait until one has time to help me, even if it feels like a long time. I don't interrupt them when they are helping someone else. I try to follow teachers' directions and remember to thank them each time they help me.

self-monitoring checklist

M	T	W	R	F	
☐	☐	☐	☐	☐	1. I use a formal greeting when I see teachers.
☐	☐	☐	☐	☐	2. I ask for help and don't demand it.
☐	☐	☐	☐	☐	3. I wait my turn.
☐	☐	☐	☐	☐	4. I follow directions.
☐	☐	☐	☐	☐	5. I thank them when they help me.

my story

M	T	W	R	F
☐	☐	☐	☐	☐
☐	☐	☐	☐	☐
☐	☐	☐	☐	☐
☐	☐	☐	☐	☐
☐	☐	☐	☐	☐

_____

_____

_____

_____

_____

six

peer relationships

skills

meeting someone new
teacher guidelines

narrative

Many students struggle with how to meet new people, whether they are adults or children their age. Often when meeting someone for the first time, some children just stand silently or feel awkward because they don't know what to say or how to act. As basic of a social skill as it is, many students have not been taught the simple etiquette of meeting new people.

Children need to know that when in a public place (e.g., school or working situation) that there is a code of social conduct which is expected. Part of the code is how to greet others and to make them feel comfortable. Students also need to know the difference between greeting an adult and a person their own age.

objective

When meeting someone new, the student will make eye contact, introduce self, listen for the other person's name and confirm meeting the person.

benchmarks

1. S will make eye contact with the new person.

2. S will introduce self by stating first and last name.

3. S will listen for the other person's name.

4. S will restate that person's name.

5. S will confirm the privilege of meeting the new person.

problem checklist

Some children from some ethnic backgrounds (e.g., Asian) may find it difficult to make eye contact because of differences in cultural attitudes. An alternative behavior can be taught instead. Children need to know the difference between meeting an adult in the school community and a peer. Teachers and other staff people should be addressed by Mr., Ms., etc., and their last name.

Some parent volunteers or older student tutors may prefer having the children use their first names.

In some social situations students need to be taught to shake hands when they meet a new person especially if the person extends a hand first.

Students can also learn how to introduce a friend or adult to a new person.

Students can learn how to respond when someone else introduces them.

teacher's script

Say, "It's important to know the right way to meet someone new, because it's something that happens a lot. When you meet someone for the first time look him in the eye, tell him your first and last name and pay attention when he tells you his name. Then say, "It was nice to meet you," and say his name back to him. People like it when you're polite about meeting them."

meeting someone new

student page

date _____

time _____

setting _____

teacher _____

period _____

student name _____

_____

self-talk story

When I meet a new student I need to try to make that person feel comfortable. I can look at her face, smile and say, "Hi my name is, (and say my name) what is your name?" I listen carefully for her name. I repeat the person's name by saying. "It's nice to meet you,"(and her name). I can offer my hand to shake or say, "If you like, I can introduce you to other students in the classroom."

self-monitoring checklist

M	T	W	R	F	
☐	☐	☐	☐	☐	1. I smile and make eye contact.
☐	☐	☐	☐	☐	2. I say the person's first and last name.
☐	☐	☐	☐	☐	3. I listen for their name.
☐	☐	☐	☐	☐	4. I say it back to them.
☐	☐	☐	☐	☐	5. I say, "it is nice to meet you."

M	T	W	R	F
☐	☐	☐	☐	☐
☐	☐	☐	☐	☐
☐	☐	☐	☐	☐
☐	☐	☐	☐	☐
☐	☐	☐	☐	☐

my story

_____

_____

_____

_____

_____

forty-one
greeting friends
teacher guidelines

narrative
Some students have difficulty starting conversations with other children, even ones they know from school or elsewhere. These students will see their friends on the sidewalks, playground, or hallways and may ignore them because they do not know how to engage them in a conversation.

Other children are so shy that they struggle with having the confidence to speak to people they know. When this happens they can gain the reputation of being aloof or rude.

objective
When the student sees a friend she will greet him by waving, smiling, or verbally acknowledging the friend.

benchmarks
1. S will wave to a friend who is at a distance.

2. S will, when encountering a friend who is near, smile and greet the person verbally.

3. When engaged in a conversation, S will speak in a normal tone of voice.

4. While talking to a friend, S will make eye contact (if culturally appropriate).

5. S is aware that the greeting may be more casual if the friendship is close.

problem checklist
Children with autism or who are extremely shy may benefit from having a social story script for how to greet friends.

Some children may have to have ways of greeting a person, which would lead to a short conversation. For example, "Hi (the person's name), how are you today?" or smile and say "Hi (the person's name)!"

Some may have to learn how far away from their friend they must stand.

Other students may not grasp the difference between greeting a good friend and someone they are merely familiar with. They need to understand that an overly friendly greeting extended to someone who is not a close friend is not appropriate and can make that person feel uncomfortable (even result in ridicule from that person).

Students need to understand that while it's appropriate to be excited about seeing a good friend, overexuberance — especially when it's public — can be offputting even to children.

teacher's script
Say, "How you greet your friends depends on if they are really good friends, or just kids you know a little. If the person is someone you know, but are not close to, smile, greet her by saying 'hi' and her name. But if she is a good friend, you may greet her in a more friendly way."

greeting friends
student page

date _____

time _____

setting _____

teacher _____

period _____

student name _____

_____

greet friends

self-talk story

When I see a friend I need to say hello in some way. If a friend is across the street or far away on the playground I can wave to her when she sees me. If I walk up to a friend I need to smile and say "Hi" (and the person's name). I need to speak in a normal voice and look at my friend's face. I can continue a conversation with my friend as we walk together.

self-monitoring checklist

M T W R F

□ □ □ □ □ 1. When I see a friend approach I wave.

□ □ □ □ □ 2. I say "hi" and the person's name.

□ □ □ □ □ 3. I use a normal voice.

□ □ □ □ □ 4. I look at the person's face.

□ □ □ □ □ 5. I know I can greet close friends in a different way.

my story

M T W R F

□ □ □ □ □ _____

□ □ □ □ □ _____

□ □ □ □ □ _____

□ □ □ □ □ _____

□ □ □ □ □ _____

joining a group of friends
teacher guidelines

narrative

Learning how to converse with friends in an age appropriate manner takes time to learn, but is a vital skill for students to master to avoid misunderstandings and to promote social success and happiness at school. However, for some students, mastering the skills for initiating conversation will require direct teacher intervention.

objective

The student will make a self-initiated attempt to join a small group situation and interact in a friendly and appropriate manner.

benchmarks

1. S will ask a group of children if it's okay to join them.

2. S will speak in a normal tone of voice.

3. S will wait for someone else to stop talking before saying something.

4. S will make comments, which are directly related to the topic.

5. S will try to include all children in the group.

problem checklist

It is hard for extremely shy children to join a group of friends in unstructured situations such as the cafeteria, playground, or informal gatherings outside the school. It is equally hard for shy children to say something when in the group. It may be necessary to break this skill down and practice statements that can be made to get the group's attention and what to say when in the group to allow shy children to use the skills in a group situation.

Some children who are by nature full of energy may tend to crowd uninvited in on a group and irritate the very kids whose company they are soliciting. These children are so eager to join that the reaction is opposite from what had been intended. Approaching the group in a calmer fashion can help you be accepted more readily by the group.

Other children may be predisposed to dominate the conversation and interrupt the person who is talking. Learning how to engage in an ongoing conversation is the target skill to emphasize for this kind of child.

Children with disabilities may struggle with impulse control issues which cause them to blurt out inappropriate statements or to act hyper in a way that irritates other children. They may need extra help with this skill for without it they will continue to experience peer alienation.

teacher's script

Say, "When you see a group of your friends, you might want to join them to play or do other things. Greet them and ask if it is okay to join them, speaking in a normal voice, not too loud. When someone else is talking, wait until they stop before you say something. Try to talk about the subject they are talking about and be nice to all the kids in the group. If you do these things, other kids will enjoy being with you and want you to join them."

joining a group of friends

student page

date _____

time _____

setting _____

teacher _____

period _____

student name _____

_____

self-talk story

I see my friends sitting at a table in the cafeteria. They look like they are already talking to each other. I walk up and ask if I can sit at the table with them. If they say yes, I sit down and thank them for letting me join. Even though the cafeteria is a large room I have to remember to talk in a classroom voice. I have to listen to the conversation and wait for my turn to speak. I show my interest by talking about the same thing. When I talk I try to look at everyone at the table so that they all feel included.

self-monitoring checklist

M T W R F

1. I ask, "May I join you?"

2. I use a normal voice.

3. I talk after the person is done talking.

4. I talk about the same topic.

5. I talk to everyone in the group.

my story

M T W R F

_____

_____

_____

_____

_____

playing with friends

teacher guidelines

narrative

While playing with friends is an important part of any child's school experience, it's frequently a cause of interpersonal social problems that can reverberate through the school day.

Conflicts with friends during recess or other leisure times can disrupt learning. Often, children with behavior problems react to these conflicts by becoming angry, aggressive or withdrawn. Those students can bring that anger into the classroom and disrupt the learning of others.

When you get stuck trying to resolve arguments between children who are friends, it may become obvious to you that students who are in conflict may lack critical social skills to play games and enjoy other activities with their friends, such as the ability to share and to compromise. These may be some of the areas in which they need some guidance.

objective

When playing with a friend the student will be able to compromise on an activity, follow the rules for that activity, take turns and demonstrate good sportsmanship.

benchmarks

1. S will compromise on an activity.

2. S will take turns when playing.

3. S will follow the rules for the game/activity.

4. S will congratulate friends for their performance.

5. S will accept losing or winning in an appropriate manner.

problem checklist

Children with poor cooperative play skills may need to have each benchmark broken down into further steps in order to be able to master cooperative play.

Some children may need a mentor, tutor, or other adult person to help supervise play situations for a short period before play skills can be self-monitored. Other students may have to have the skills reviewed before recess for several days in order to help foreshadow what is expected when they play with friends.

Some students might struggle with the concept of "compromise." Ask them if they know what it means, and if necessary, explain.

teacher's script

Say, "It's fun to play with your friends on the playground. But when you play together it's important to play fair and to share and compromise. If you don't do these things, sometimes you get in fights and you are still mad when you go into the school. Then you have a bad day. When you play fair and compromise, you and your friends have a good time."

playing with friends

student page

playing with a friend

date _____

time _____

setting _____

teacher _____

period _____

student name _____

_____

self-talk story

It is time for recess. I want to play a game, but my friend wants to play a different game. We decide to compromise. This is what we will do: Sometimes we will play her favorite game, sometimes we will play mine. We will take turns.

When playing with my friend I wait my turn. I follow the rules. I remember to compliment my friend on the way she played. I remember that playing with my friend is more important than winning or losing.

self-monitoring checklist

M T W R F

1. I agree on what we are going to play.

2. I take turns with my friends.

3. I stick to the rules.

4. I praise others for their skills.

5. I enjoy when I win and accept when I lose.

my story

M T W R F

_____

_____

_____

_____

_____

forty-four
starting conversations
teacher guidelines

narrative

Some students have a hard time initiating conversation because they don't get the social rules for engaging others in an appropriate conversation. As a result these children will often make "off the wall" comments just to attract attention. This accomplishes the regrettable purpose of getting them attention which is often negative.

Other students are shy and wait for friends to initiate a conversation because they lack the skills to start one themselves. Regular instruction and practice of conversational skills is a must for these students.

objective

The student will make self-initiated attempts to engage a friend in a conversation using appropriate eye contact and listening skills.

benchmarks

1. S thinks about what to say before talking to a friend.

2. S initiates conversation with a proper greeting.

3. S listens to the friend and maintains eye contact

4. S waits for friend to finish before talking again.

5. When the conversation is over, S says good-bye and walks away.

problem checklist

Some students with a history of poor peer interactions may need guided practice before they begin to converse on their own. Guided practice can take place in the form of role-plays or written social stories. While it may be that these children are able to recite the rules for a conversation, they haven't mastered them and can't use them consistently in conversations. They need to be taught social interaction skills much the same as they would learn reading skills and they need to practice them in a simulated context.

teacher's script

Say, "Sometimes it's hard to start a conversation with other kids. It helps if you think about what you want to say before you say it and if you listen carefully to what they say to you before you say something back to them."

122

starting conversations

student page

date _____

time _____

setting _____

teacher _____

period _____

student name _____

_____

learning to start a conversation

self-talk story

I see someone I want to talk to. As I walk up to him I think about what I am going to say. I say, "Hi (the person's name), how are you?" I wait for him to finish talking before speaking again. Then I tell him what it was I thought about saying. Maybe I want to do something with him, or just introduce myself. When he talks to me, I look directly at him. I wait until he finishes talking and then I say something to him. When it is time to go, I say, "Good-bye, (his name) I'll see you later!"

self-monitoring checklist

M	T	W	R	F	
☐	☐	☐	☐	☐	1. I say "Hi" and the person's name.
☐	☐	☐	☐	☐	2. I decide what to talk about.
☐	☐	☐	☐	☐	3. I listen and look at the person.
☐	☐	☐	☐	☐	4. I wait until the person is done.
☐	☐	☐	☐	☐	5. I say "goodbye" when we part.

my story

M	T	W	R	F
☐	☐	☐	☐	☐
☐	☐	☐	☐	☐
☐	☐	☐	☐	☐
☐	☐	☐	☐	☐
☐	☐	☐	☐	☐

_____

_____

_____

_____

_____

respecting friends

teacher guidelines

narrative

Friendships are essential to most children. Some students are well liked and have many friends; some only a few and are satisfied to have just a best friend.

Other children are able to make friends but struggle with keeping them over a long period of time. These students can become anxious or sad when friendships fall apart. They can perceive themselves as not being very likeable or come to think there is something seriously wrong with them. This type of student benefits from learning rules for respecting friendships and specific ways to maintain compatibility and trust.

objective

The student will show respect to friends by greeting them properly, including them in activities, sharing play or school materials, thanking them when appropriate and addressing them at all times in a respectful manner.

benchmarks

1. S will greet friends using their name when in public places.

2. S will introduce friends to others and include them in play activities.

3. S will share play or school materials.

4. S will thank the friend for help or a gift.

5. S will talk in a respectful manner to the friend.

problem checklist

Children who cannot keep friendships often do not understand that their friends need to be treated the same way as they expect to be treated themselves. For example, some children need to be reminded not to yell out personal nicknames in large public area such as the cafeteria, unless it is one the friend doesn't mind others knowing.

Students with impulse control issues in general have a spotty history of friendships and need some internal governance in this area.

Some children may need to rehearse a social script for sharing play and school materials and taking turns during activities. Often children forget to thank friends for helping them out with something. It's just as important to thank friends as it is adults.

Others may need to practice how to talk to their friends so that they don't monopolize a play situation or seem too bossy. You may need to write very specific scripts for individual children depending upon what it is that they need to learn.

teacher's script

Say, "Most of us want to have friends who like and respect us. We need to remember that they want us to respect them too. I will remember to thank my friends when they help me, share my things with them when they ask and always treat them with respect like they treat me."

respecting friends

student page

learning to respect friends

date _____

time _____

setting _____

teacher _____

period _____

student name _____

_____

self-talk story

I see my friends at school. I greet them with respect and introduce them to others if they haven't already met them. I offer to give them help if they need it, or ask them for help if I do. When they help me, I thank them. If they do something well, I compliment them on their skill. That makes them smile and feel good and they enjoy doing things with me.

M T W R F
☐ ☐ ☐ ☐ ☐
☐ ☐ ☐ ☐ ☐
☐ ☐ ☐ ☐ ☐
☐ ☐ ☐ ☐ ☐
☐ ☐ ☐ ☐ ☐

self-monitoring checklist

1. I greet friends with respect.

2. I introduce them to others.

3. I share with them.

4. I thank them when they help me.

5. I compliment them for good things they do.

M T W R F
☐ ☐ ☐ ☐ ☐
☐ ☐ ☐ ☐ ☐
☐ ☐ ☐ ☐ ☐
☐ ☐ ☐ ☐ ☐
☐ ☐ ☐ ☐ ☐

my story

_____

_____

_____

_____

_____

being a good sport

teacher guidelines

narrative

Good sportsmanship involves playing by the rules of a game and encouraging others on their performance. But sportsmanship doesn't just apply to team sports. It includes any competitive activity, such as board games, games like tag, cards and even use of playground equipment that requires sharing.

When involved in game-like activities sometimes it's easy for students to forget that winning or being the best at an activity isn't always the goal of the game. Learning to lose without pouting or protesting is a hard lesson for some children. Complimenting others on their abilities is an important interactive skill that needs to be developed, as opposed to taunting or arguing about another's ability "to win."

objective

When playing a game the student will follow the rules and compliment others on their skills.

benchmarks

1. S follows the rules of the game.

2. S gives others an opportunity to participate in the game.

3. S compliments other players during the game.

4. S compliments the other person or team if they win the game.

5. S accepts winning or losing in a gracious manner.

problem checklist

Children see winning as the primary goal of a competition. While winning is certainly an enjoyable experience, students need to understand that playing according to the rules and savoring the experience of the game are also ways of winning.

Conflicts at recess can occur because a student or small group of students try to win by breaking rules or making up their own rules in order to win. For these children it may be necessary to write a sequence that teaches sportsmanship and how to play a game according to the rules.

Learning to share and to take turns are hard skills. Some students may need to focus on sharing and taking turns before they can develop the skill of complimenting others or learning how to win and lose gracefully.

teacher's script

Say, "When you play games with your friends it's important to be a good sport, even if you lose. When the game is over, you should tell the other players that they did a good job. Then they will want to play with you again."

being a good sport

student page

date _____

time _____

setting _____

teacher _____

period _____

student name _____

_____

learning to be a good sport

self-talk story

I like to play games with my friends. I practiced hard and I have learned the rules of the game so that I am good at it. I have to remember that it is a group game and I have to be sure that everyone has a chance to play. When I see an opportunity I include another players to help our team. When someone else makes a good play I shout "Way to go (and their name)!" If our team wins I try to shake the other players' hands and say "thank you" when they tell me my team played well.

self-monitoring checklist

M	T	W	R	F	
☐	☐	☐	☐	☐	1. I follow the game rules.
☐	☐	☐	☐	☐	2. I give others a chance.
☐	☐	☐	☐	☐	3. I compliment players on my team.
☐	☐	☐	☐	☐	4. I compliment the other team.
☐	☐	☐	☐	☐	5. I enjoy when I win and accept when I lose.

my story

M	T	W	R	F
☐	☐	☐	☐	☐
☐	☐	☐	☐	☐
☐	☐	☐	☐	☐
☐	☐	☐	☐	☐
☐	☐	☐	☐	☐

_____

_____

_____

_____

_____

forty-seven
dealing with bullies
teacher guidelines

narrative

Students should never feel uncomfortable about coming to school because of fears of being bullied, excessively teased, or harassed. Yet, many children at one point or another find themselves in a situation where they are confronted by a bully.

However, students also need to learn the difference between inappropriate teasing and actual bullying. Teachers need to determine the differences between teasing and harassment. Helping students empower themselves helps build skills for learning how to deal with confrontations. Teaching children to stick up for themselves, to walk towards a group of friends, use good judgment when alone with a bully, telling an adult as soon as soon as possible, and getting out of the bullies' way are strategies which can help.

It is worth considering peer mediation if it is available in your district.

objective

When confronted by a bully the student will develop and implement a strategy for dealing with the bully.

benchmarks

1. S tells an adult about the times that he/she is bullied.

2. S develops a strategy with a trusted person to deter the bully.

3. S practices the strategy with a trusted person. (Walks with confidence, avoids being alone with the bully tells an adult when he/she is bullied and uses humor to deflect threats.)

4. S uses the strategy.

5. S assesses the success and modifies the strategy if necessary.

problem checklist

Often a teacher needs to confront the bully and find out the reasons why it is occurring. In extreme cases, administrators and parents may need to be involved. Once the teacher has an understanding of the situation, a plan can be developed and practiced with the child who is trying to avoid being bullied.

In addition, consequences need to be developed for the child who continues to bully because no one has the right to make someone else feel unsafe. Bullies need to be taught more appropriate ways of interacting with other people.

It also must be noted that interventions serve the bully as well as his victim, since bullies are often marginalized by their antisocial behavior. Role play rehearsals of the student's plan, both with adults and with a peer (usually a friend of the child) help to strengthen the efficacy of child's strategy.

teacher's script

Say, "Nobody likes to be bullied, but it happens a lot at school so you may need to have a plan to deal with it. If it's happening to you, you can tell an adult you trust and ask for help. There are some simple things you can do with a good plan that will protect you."

dealing with bullies

dealing with bullies

date _____

time _____

setting _____

teacher _____

period _____

student name _____

_____

self-talk story

I feel uncomfortable and anxious whenever I see a bully because it makes me feel unsafe. I talked to my teacher and we thought of a plan to deal with it. I practiced the plan with my teacher and a friend. If the plan doesn't work, I will get help to make another plan until I find one that does.

M	T	W	R	F
☐	☐	☐	☐	☐
☐	☐	☐	☐	☐
☐	☐	☐	☐	☐
☐	☐	☐	☐	☐
☐	☐	☐	☐	☐

self-monitoring checklist

1. I tell a friend or adult.

2. I make a plan to deal with it.

3. I practice my plan.

4. I use my plan.

5. If it doesn't work, I make another plan.

M	T	W	R	F
☐	☐	☐	☐	☐
☐	☐	☐	☐	☐
☐	☐	☐	☐	☐
☐	☐	☐	☐	☐
☐	☐	☐	☐	☐

my story

_____

_____

_____

_____

_____

dealing with conflicts
teacher guidelines

narrative

Conflicts between students are inevitable. Learning how to deal with them is critical. This is best understood as a sophisticated, but vital, skill. Perhaps, the best way to approach it is to teach children a variety of ways to manage conflicts so they can always find one which fits the situation and resolves the problem.

Strategies to discuss with the students include: Talking directly to the person with whom the student has a conflict; using humor; staying calm; compromising, looking at the person in the eye and saying, " Stop that I don't like it," and walking away; walking towards a group of friends if they are near by; and telling a friend or an adult about the problem. These are but a few strategies which can be taught.

Eventually children learn as they mature what strategies work best for them when they are trying to avoid conflicts. The sooner they start this process, the better.

In addition, students and teachers should be aware of the sometimes subtle differences between managing minor conflicts and bullying.

objective

Will develop and follow a plan for managing conflicts.

benchmarks

1. S verbalizes what led to the conflict.

2. S tries to (with guidance from the teacher) understand both sides of the conflict.

3. S brainstorms to prevent the conflict from occurring.

4. S follows a plan.

5. S tries another plan if the first one doesn't work.

problem checklist

As we said above, there are some occasions in which in it appropriate to tell adults about a problem. But there always some students who run to adults to "tattle" about another child's behavior. Instead of always expecting the adult to solve a conflict these children need to learn the difference between minor problems and serious conflicts. Children who constantly use adults as their only plan to deal with conflicts become limited in their ability to resolve problems and risk gaining a reputation as a "tattle-tale." Eventually they will become isolated from other students for lack of trust.

Children who are bullies and initiate conflicts throughout the school day need adults to supervise a conflict resolution plan. These students need extra practice on how to behave so that conflicts are lessened.

teacher's script

Say, "Conflicts happen when two people disagree about something. When this happens your feelings can get hurt or the person you are fighting with will get hurt. This won't happen if you have a smart plan to avoid conflicts."

dealing with conflicts

student page

date _____

time _____

setting _____

teacher _____

period _____

student name _____

_____

learning to avoid conflicts

self-talk story

I don't want to get into an argument or fight with other kids but it's hard not to. I try to ignore these situations but sometimes that plan doesn't work. I talked to my teacher and decided to use another plan. I will try it and if it doesn't work I can talk to my teacher about another plan. I will keep trying until I find one that works.

self-monitoring checklist

M	T	W	R	F	
☐	☐	☐	☐	☐	1. I know what the conflict is.
☐	☐	☐	☐	☐	2. I try to see the other person's side.
☐	☐	☐	☐	☐	3. I talk about the conflict with someone.
☐	☐	☐	☐	☐	4. I make and follow a plan to deal with it.
☐	☐	☐	☐	☐	5. If it doesn't work, I make another plan.

my story

M	T	W	R	F
☐	☐	☐	☐	☐
☐	☐	☐	☐	☐
☐	☐	☐	☐	☐
☐	☐	☐	☐	☐
☐	☐	☐	☐	☐

_____

_____

_____

_____

_____

compromising
teacher guidelines

narrative

Children who know how to compromise and demonstrate a sportsmanship-like attitude during group activities are more accepted by their classmates than those who do not possess these skills.

With the decrease in neighborhood outdoor games and more organized sport activities some children have less of an opportunity to learn how to negotiate compromises on their own.

For other students winning is the goal, or an insistence on playing their favorite position in a game is more important than negotiating with their friends. Children who always insist on having their own way are perceived as being bossy or selfish.

Children who do not possess a "give and take" attitude can feel isolated or not liked. Some mask their feeling by being too aggressive. It is important to assess whether or not a child has had enough opportunities to learn how to compromise or whether it is a compulsive attempt to control the situation. Children who are aggressive can use this behavior to hide the fact that they do not have the skills to compromise with their friends. These students may need a step-by-step procedure on how to negotiate in a less threatening manner.

objective

When in a group activity the student will follow a plan to compromise with other children.

benchmarks

1. S will use a strategy that lends itself to compromise (e.g., taking turns at an activity or position).
2. S chooses an activity based upon the compromise.
3. S helps decide roles (or positions) for each person.
4. S follows the rules of the compromise.
5. S congratulates other people on their play skills.

problem checklist

Students who have not had the opportunity to problem-solve conflicts on their own may need adult guidance on the ways that one can compromise when in conflict during a group activity. This comes under the heading of "basic life skill." Students need to be encouraged to develop their own strategies rather than always relying upon an adult to give them one. They are more likely to adhere to the compromise if it is one that comes from them.

For children who always insist on winning, giving them a chance to teach or "referee" a group of younger students can give them a leadership role that they seem to desire, which in turn provides a lesson in the role of fair play. Teaching them how to negotiate compromise with the younger students can lead to helping them learn strategies to use with their own peers.

teacher's script

Say, "It's important to learn how to compromise with your friends and other kids when you're playing games or sharing playground equipment. When you can compromise, everybody gets to take part and you don't get into fights with other kids."

compromising

student page

learning to compromise

date _____

time _____

setting _____

teacher _____

period _____

student name _____

_____

self-talk story

At recess I am practicing my skills so I can be better at my favorite game. I try to play other games too because my friends might have different favorite games than I do. When we play a game together, I try to share the ball and play by the rules of the game. I know I have to share my favorite position, because other kids like to play it too. I remember to congratulate my friends and other kids for playing a good game.

self-monitoring checklist

M	T	W	R	F	
☐	☐	☐	☐	☐	1. I know why I need to compromise.
☐	☐	☐	☐	☐	2. I try to see the other person's side.
☐	☐	☐	☐	☐	3. I talk to the person about it.
☐	☐	☐	☐	☐	4. I help the other person make a plan.
☐	☐	☐	☐	☐	5. I follow the plan.

my story

M	T	W	R	F
☐	☐	☐	☐	☐
☐	☐	☐	☐	☐
☐	☐	☐	☐	☐
☐	☐	☐	☐	☐
☐	☐	☐	☐	☐

_____

_____

_____

_____

_____

showing empathy
teacher guidelines

narrative

Elementary school students are often very caring and empathetic. It's not unusual to see a group of children gathered around a hurt comrade on the playground, or to express a willingness to assist a classmate who is ill to the nurse's office. Part of the joy of teaching young children is that they demonstrate such caring.

But some children who are extremely withdrawn or angry may have difficulty showing empathy toward other students. Often these children feel the same concern but are unable to communicate it to others. Tragically, they often gain a reputation for not caring because they give out few expressions of empathy. For some it becomes hard to break out of their role as "tough guy" because it's a safe and comfortable way for them to keep interaction with others at a minimum. It can be challenging to teach these kinds of young people how to show empathy for others, but it's vital that they do, or their classmates will continue to avoid them.

objective

Will express concerns about another person's hurt feelings.

benchmarks

1. S will recognize the facial expression or body language of a person who is feeling sad or hurt.

2. S will attempt to understand how his/her friend feels in a particular situation.

3. S will offer to help or support a friend in some manner.

4. S will speak in a soft and caring voice.

5. If the friend is not willing to accept help, S will wait and try again later.

problem checklist

Showing empathy is another essential skill that can be very difficult for some young students to learn. One way to help students understand the hurt of classmates is to remind them of a time they felt sad. Even elementary school students who are naturally caring may need suggestions on how to help friends who are feeling hurt. Verbal support is important but students can show other ways of helping friends, too. A written note or e-mail works when friends are not ready to talk about why they feel down.

Including friends in activities, such as a game at recess or joining a group of lunch buddies to eat in the cafeteria are ways to show support without directly talking about an incident or a feeling. Students should wait until their friends are ready to discuss the causes of their feelings.

Students also need to know that if the friend is unwilling to talk about the problem, it's not a reflection on the friendship. Some children struggle with revealing their emotions. When this is the case, students wishing to show support need to know that their attempts are probably very appreciated.

teacher's script

Say, "When you have friends who feel really bad about something, you need to show you care about their feelings. Ask them if there's anything you can do to help, but understand if they're not ready to talk about it yet. When you show them you care, it makes them feel better and you feel better too."

showing empathy

student page

learning to show empathy

date _____

time _____

setting _____

teacher _____

period _____

student name _____

_____

self-talk story

When my friends seem upset, I can tell because they act differently. They don't smile as much and sometimes they don't talk and they try to avoid me. I will try to help them feel better by asking what the problem is and if they want to talk about it, I'd be happy to listen. Sometimes they are ready to talk, but if they aren't I understand and wait until later.

M	T	W	R	F
☐	☐	☐	☐	☐
☐	☐	☐	☐	☐
☐	☐	☐	☐	☐
☐	☐	☐	☐	☐
☐	☐	☐	☐	☐

self-monitoring checklist

1. I know why I need to show empathy.

2. I know what it's like to be hurt.

3. I ask about the problem in a calm voice.

4. I know the person may not be able to deal with it.

5. If the person needs more time, I ask again later.

M	T	W	R	F
☐	☐	☐	☐	☐
☐	☐	☐	☐	☐
☐	☐	☐	☐	☐
☐	☐	☐	☐	☐
☐	☐	☐	☐	☐

my story

_____

_____

_____

_____

_____

Three Super Social Skills

introduction

51. following directions
52. being compliant
53. accepting others

The three skills in this section are essential to having a classroom community that feels comfortable to all members. They are core behaviors that will shape your class into a learning environment instead of one where you have to discipline constantly. Your students will require these skills in
many different situations throughout the day.

It is critical that you address the behaviors of students who either can't follow directions, refuse to comply, or exclude others based upon how they look or act. (Children who bully or threaten other students are another issue altogether. They need to be taught more acceptable ways of interacting. A child's safety is always an overriding concern and must be dealt with on its own.)

As with the first 50 social skills it is important to pinpoint the student's performance on these skills in your informal assessments. Don't assume that a student can follow directions just because he or she isn't a behavior problem. Teaching students how to follow directions and comply with teacher requests allows them to gain attention in a more acceptable way. In addition, it allows them to develop confidence and reduces the chance they will feel threatened by teacher requests.

Accepting others who are different because of a physical feature, economic status or a learning problem allows a child to learn how to be more tolerant in a community with many different people. The goal here is not to force friendships on your students with kids who may be significantly different, but rather to accept the differences and to prevent them using these children as a target for teasing or exclusion. Accepting others with differences will make your students feel better about themselves and will improve their chances of adapting in an increasingly diversified society.

137

following directions

teacher guidelines

narrative

Following directions is an essential skill. Consider the number of times throughout the school day a student is given directions. If a child doesn't understand, which isn't uncommon among students with disabilities, he is unable to follow through on teacher expectations. Not following through is often confused by staff as oppositional behavior on the part of the student.

Many times students with disabilities learn better visually or by using tactile kinesthetic materials. However, directions are often given orally without visual cues. By posting them in the room the child has a constant visual cue as to what the rules are.

In addition, teachers need to instruct all students in basic school and classroom rules, since directions are a reiteration of those rules in action. At the beginning of the year, review class and school rules thoroughly. Review them continually throughout the year.

objective

When given direction, S will stop what she is doing, look at the teacher, listen to the direction and comply with what has been said.

benchmarks

1. When the teacher starts to talk, S stops what she is doing.

2. When the teacher is speaking, S will look at the teacher.

3. S will be quiet while the teacher is talking.

4. S will use other students as models on how to comply.

5. S will ask to clarify a direction and comply as soon as she understands what to do.

problem checklist

Children with autism and children from different cultures may have difficulty looking at a teacher or maintaining eye contact. Encourage these children to look in the direction of the teacher or make fleeting eye contact so you know the child is trying to listen. Reinforce compliance to that direction so the student understands how to respond to oral instructions. Praise for student effort helps promote behavior that leads towards proficiency. For example: "Ariana, thank you for stopping your work to listen to me." Whenever possible reinforce oral directions with written directions or some kind of visual schedule, so when a student forgets, there is a concrete reminder for her to reference. Encourage students to model off others who don't struggle with this, and to look at and follow them when they are confused. For students who have a tendency to blurt, reinforce raising hands for help. Some students will benefit from repeating the direction quietly back to themselves so other students are not distracted.

teacher's script

Say, "It's hard to remember all the directions I give to my class. Here are some strategies you can use to follow them. When I say 'class I need your attention,' stop your work and look at me. If you are quiet and listen, it will help you remember what I said. If you forget, look at the other students and use them as a cue for what you need to do, or raise your hand and I will help you."

following directions

student page

date _____

time _____

setting _____

teacher _____

period _____

student name _____

_____

self-talk story

I need to listen to adults when I am given a direction. When my teacher tells the class to listen, I tell myself to stop what I am doing and look at her. I wait until she is done before I raise my hand to ask a question. When I have trouble remembering, I watch my classmates. I try to copy what they are doing. I feel proud when I follow directions and my teacher smiles at me.

self-monitoring checklist

M	T	W	R	F	
☐	☐	☐	☐	☐	1. I stop what I am doing.
☐	☐	☐	☐	☐	2. I look at adults and listen to their directions.
☐	☐	☐	☐	☐	3. I watch how others do it.
☐	☐	☐	☐	☐	4. If I don't understand, I ask for help
☐	☐	☐	☐	☐	5. I do what is asked.

my story

M	T	W	R	F
☐	☐	☐	☐	☐
☐	☐	☐	☐	☐
☐	☐	☐	☐	☐
☐	☐	☐	☐	☐
☐	☐	☐	☐	☐

_____

_____

_____

_____

_____

being compliant
teacher guidelines

narrative

Being compliant around adults is an important skill to develop to build interpersonal skills. Compliance is more than just being able to follow oral directions. It's a response to the social rules for interacting with others. Students must comply with adult requests (and sometimes peers) to be able to have constructive interactions within the school community. When teaching compliance, focus on behaviors a child must learn rather than ones she is exhibiting. This will help you avoid circular arguments and getting into power struggles. A student who does not understand the rules for compliance must be taught these skills the same way one would teach an academic concept.

objective

The student will comply with teacher requests.

benchmarks

1. When name is called, S will respond by looking at the teacher.

2. S will respond verbally to an adult

3. S will respond to a single direction by the teacher.

4. S will accept adult direction.

5. S will act on adult direction.

problem checklist

Students who struggle with compliance may not understand the complexities of many social interactions. Resistant students may be unwilling to give up what they see as control to another individual. Rather than to respond to a request, they may argue or simply refuse. Students who quickly become oppositional are frustrating, and don't respond well to threats or power statements. Nor do point systems teach skills to develop more appropriate ways of responding. They are rarely effective with oppositional students.

Instead, use a shaping technique to teach compliance. For example, a verbal response may need to start with a single word answer. The teacher can then help the student expand to a phrase and finally an age appropriate sentence. A single direction is just that, the most minimal response the student must make to comply. Reinforce the behavior and talk about what the child needs to do. Ignore the "no" response some children automatically give and wait for them to comply before repeating the direction. Some children will say no but eventually will comply. For example, Joe doesn't like to read in large group and refuses to get out the reading text or makes noises so other students are distracted. Negotiate a behavior that allows him to participate in the group without distracting other children: Such as, he doesn't need to read out loud and won't be called on but must sit quietly and follow while others read.

Giving a non-compliant child a role in helping others such as passing out papers, collecting books, being the leader in the line, or taking a message to the office allows the student to be responsible and complaint with class rules.

teacher's script

Say, "When I ask you to do something you need to follow my requests. If you look at me and respond by saying 'Yes (and my name),' it will help you to pay attention to what I'm asking you to do. If you don't know how to do what I ask, let me know by raising your hand,"

being compliant

student page

being
compliant

date _____

time _____

setting _____

teacher _____

period _____

student name _____

_____

self-talk story

I try to participate in class and to be accepted by my teacher and friends. But sometimes it is hard for me to do what my teacher asks me to do. My teacher and I have come up with a plan so that I feel more comfortable in the classroom. My plan will help me learn.

M T W R F

☐ ☐ ☐ ☐ ☐
☐ ☐ ☐ ☐ ☐
☐ ☐ ☐ ☐ ☐
☐ ☐ ☐ ☐ ☐
☐ ☐ ☐ ☐ ☐

self-monitoring checklist

1. I stop and look at adults speaking to me.

2. I speak politely to adults.

3. If I don't understand, I ask for help.

4. I say I will obey.

5. I act on the adult request.

M T W R F

☐ ☐ ☐ ☐ ☐
☐ ☐ ☐ ☐ ☐
☐ ☐ ☐ ☐ ☐
☐ ☐ ☐ ☐ ☐
☐ ☐ ☐ ☐ ☐

my story

_____

_____

_____

_____

_____

accepting others
teacher guidelines

narrative

Most elementary school students are eager to help others who look different or struggle with learning. Young children are often more accepting of individual differences than adults. However, there are exceptions. Students who seem different can become the subject of teasing from classmates. The teacher must address that child's needs and teach appropriate skills to students who are teasing and making put downs.

Targets for teasing or derogatory remarks include kids who are: Overweight, have reading disabilities, poor social interactions or come from disadvantaged families. These are not things students have control over. Hurtful statements continue to make them feel left out. Students who tease others for innate differences must learn skills so they don't torment others. Acceptance means developing skills to prevent them from discrimination based on individual differences.

objective

The student will learn skills that will assist him/her to accept individual differences.

benchmarks

1. S will use a normal tone of voice when speaking to others.

2. S will use appreciations or praise when appropriate instead of put downs or embarrassing statements.

3. S will include others in conversations or group activities.

4. S will be able to identify ways other people can be hurt

5. S will accept others despite individual differences.

problem checklist

Students need alternative ways to relate to children who are different. Encourage them to make statements which are supportive, or at least neutral. Allowing students to come up with their own statements makes it more natural for them instead of putting adult statements in their mouths.

Looking at or nodding one's head in response to what a child is saying is one small step towards accepting that child. Instead of shrinking away, students can use appropriate body space with that child when in a group. Teaching small ways to show acceptance is easier for a child to accomplish. In addition, assist students in learning to identify ways of interacting that can be hurtful to others. Ask students to prepare a short list of words and behaviors that hurts their feelings. Once they have identified things that hurt them, they understand how they might hurt others.

The goal is not to teach friendships but to familiarize students with the concepts of tolerance and acceptance. That process will help everyone feel part of the classroom community and to help individual students become more sensitive towards physical attributes, academic skills and unique behaviors.

teacher's script

Say, "It's okay to like people for different reasons. You like your best friend in a different way than your other friends. But it can be hard to accept people who look and talk different than you. It's important to talk to all students in a way that doesn't hurt their feelings. When you are kind to students who are different from you, it makes them feel good and you feel good, too."

accepting others

student page

date _____

time _____

setting _____

teacher _____

period _____

student name _____

_____

accepting others

self-talk story

I don't like it when other people make fun of me. It hurts my feelings. I am trying not to hurt other people's feelings because I know that it can make them unhappy. Here is my plan so that I do not hurt other people's feelings.

M T W R F

☐ ☐ ☐ ☐ ☐
☐ ☐ ☐ ☐ ☐
☐ ☐ ☐ ☐ ☐
☐ ☐ ☐ ☐ ☐
☐ ☐ ☐ ☐ ☐

self-monitoring checklist

1. I use a normal voice when speaking to others.

2. I compliment others and don't say things that embarrass them.

3. I include others in work groups or conversations.

4. I know put-downs hurt people's feelings.

5. I accept others, even people who are different.

M T W R F

☐ ☐ ☐ ☐ ☐
☐ ☐ ☐ ☐ ☐
☐ ☐ ☐ ☐ ☐
☐ ☐ ☐ ☐ ☐
☐ ☐ ☐ ☐ ☐

my story

_____

_____

_____

_____

_____

seven
resources

1. introductory letter
2. home report
3. progress report
4. skill assessment sheet
5. sequence assessment sheet
6. benchmark goals
7. skill goals
8. sequence goals

introductory letter

Date _____

Dear _____,

_____ will soon begin a program called Social Standards in School. This program teaches 53 social skills that are important for your child to have to experience success and happiness in school.

Social Standards promotes independence and competency in such basic social skills as Asking for Help, Dealing with Bullies and Responding to Teasing. Complex skills are included, like Making an Apology and Accepting Criticism.

As your child makes progress in this program, he/she will be asked to "self-monitor" his/her improvements. This means he/she will chart his/her own progress on a form provided for him/her. Your child will carry these forms around with him/her as part of a student "portfolio." Sharing his/her forms with you can be a helpful part of his/her progress and for this reason he/she will be encouraged to bring this portfolio home to share with you.

Included with this letter is a progress report listing the 53 skills on which your child will be assessed. Each skill is made up of five steps, or Benchmarks, which will be included in the portfolio your child will bring home.

I appreciate any help you are able to give me.

Cordially, _____

_____
phone

home report

notes from school	date

skill

notes from home	date

skill

notes from school	date

skill

notes from home	date

skill

resources

progress report

student _____

instructor _____

social skills
getting ready

	date	rating	date	rating	date	rating
1. getting ready for school						
2. walking to school						
3. waiting for the bus						
4. riding the bus						
5. arriving by car						

transitions

6. transition into the building						
7. individual transitions						
8. going to the IMC						
9. being in specials						
10. standing in line						
11. transition into specials						
12. group transition						
13. going to the office						
14. checking out of school						

classroom

15. visitor to the classroom						
16. one-on-one						
17. large group activities						
18. transitions in class						
19. quiet time						
20. small group activities						
21. getting organized						
22. class jobs						

breaks & special events

23. lunch break						
24. eating skills						
25. coming in from recess						
26. knowing recess rules						
27. crisis drills						

rating key: ✚ can do independently   − in training   ✗ can't perform the activity but not in training   ☐ not applicable

progress report

semester _____

comments _____

social skills

	date	rating	date	rating	date	rating
28. going to the nurse						
29. field trips						
30. going to the bathroom *anyplace*						
31. greeting teachers						
32. asking for help						
33. respecting body space						
34. responding to teasing						
35. being responsible						
36. making an apology						
37. voice volume						
38. accepting criticism						
39. respecting teachers						

peer relationships

	date	rating	date	rating	date	rating
40. meeting someone new						
41. greeting friends						
42. joining a group of friends						
43. playing with friends						
44. starting conversations						
45. respecting friends						
46. being a good sport						
47. dealing with bullies						
48. dealing with conflicts						
49. compromising						
50. showing empathy						
51. following directions						
52. being compliant						
53. accepting others						

rating key: **+** can do independently **−** in training **x** can't perform the activity but not in training ☐ not applicable

skill assessment sheet

skill _____ student _____

skill # _____

	benchmarks	date	date	date	date	date
1.	_____					
2.	_____					
3.	_____					
4.	_____					
5.	_____					

rating key: [✦] well done   [–] poorly done   [✘] did not do   [ ] not applicable

comments _____

_____

_____

_____

_____

_____

_____

goal set _____ review _____
                    date   date

resources

sequence assessment sheet

student _____

skills	date	date	date	date	date
1. _____					
2. _____					
3. _____					
4. _____					
5. _____					
6. _____					
7. _____					
8. _____					

rating key: [✦] well done   [−] poorly done   [𝒙] did not do   [ ] not applicable

comments _____
_____
_____
_____
_____
_____
_____
_____

goal set _____   review _____
            date   date

benchmark goals

date _____

_____ will learn to _____.
              name   benchmark

This benchmark is needed for _____.
                                           skill

It will be practiced in _____ in which it naturally occurs.
                                location

Successful completion of the benchmark is defined by performing the behavior

_____.

comments _____

_____

_____

_____

_____

_____

_____

skill goals

date _____

_____ will _____
name   skill

by _____. Success is defined by completing at least _____ out
date

of _____ benchmarks. Presently he can do _____ benchmarks correctly.
quantity

comments _____

_____

_____

_____

_____

_____

_____

sequence goals

date _____

_____ will be able to complete this sequence of
                    name

_____ by
                    skills

_____ at ___ out of ___ times.

These skills have been sequenced because _____

_____.

comments _____

_____

_____

_____

_____

_____

_____

_____

_____